The author wishes to express his thanks and appreciation to the following who granted permission to use the following material:

Martin Luther King, Jr. Foundation for permission to use "I Have A Dream," © 1963,
Lawrence Freidman for permission to use "A History of American Law," © 1973

What others are saying about this book:

"This book is the best resource I've acquired all year and my self-confidence is up as a result of Michael's class. I was so pumped up I changed all my voice mail messages the first night! I know it will make me a better person both personally and professionally. The results have exceeded my expectations." *-Jimmy Bradley, Senior Information Systems Manager, St. Jude Children's Research Hospital*

"Twelve Secrets Of A Great Voice moves along well, no fluff or dull information. The exercises are fun and have helped me improve my presentation skills immensely. I now know why Michael's classes and seminars fill up so quickly. He is hot! Every speaker should own a copy of this book and attend his seminars!" *- David Jennings, ATM, President Jennings & Associates, member-Toastmasters International*

"Michael's book is wonderful! It picks up where others have left off in voice training. His methods are practical and the goals are easily attainable. Now I don't fear speaking in public as much because I am developing a great voice!" *- Kathy Starnes, Vice-President Century Properties, Inc.*

"Any speaker or trainer wishing to take his or her presentations to the next level should read this book. I'm glad I finally found a practical 'How-To' on voice training written by an accomplished speaking professional. I especially love the mouth aerobics and storytelling techniques. Michael's key points will help anyone convey their message more effectively." *- Susan Davis, Professional Trainer and Consultant The Davis-Nelson Group, member-National Speakers Association*

Twelve Secrets Of A Great Voice

TWELVE SECRETS
OF A GREAT VOICE

A PRACTICAL GUIDE FOR
ENHANCING YOUR PRESENTATIONS,
CAREER & LIFE

To Dietmar —
Best Wishes for Success!
Michael W. Hall

MICHAEL W. HALL

CCI PUBLISHING • CORDOVA

TWELVE SECRETS OF A GREAT VOICE

A Practical Guide for Enhancing Your Presentations, Career & Life

Copyright © 1997 by Michael W. Hall

Graphics and Page Design: John Childress
Cover Design: John Childress/JC Designs

Library of Congress Catalog Card Number: 97-65986
Hall, Michael W.
Twelve Secrets Of A Great Voice; a practical guide for enhancing
your presentations, career & life / by Michael W. Hall. 1st ed.

p. cm.
ISBN 1-890432-22-9 (pbk.)
1. Communication
2. Self-actualization/Self-help
3. Business presentations
4. Public Speaking
5. Education & Teaching
658.4'53--dc20 1997.

                                        97-65986
                                          CCN

Published by:

676 Germantown Parkway, Suite 538
Cordova, TN 38018 U.S.A.
1-800-989-2013

CCI
PUBLISHING
"Leaders In Progressive
Publishing"

Printed in the United States of America
10 9 8 7 6 5 4 3 2 1

Preface

This book was written for those who want to improve the quality of their presentations through the power of the spoken word. I have been wanting to provide a resource such as this for speakers, seminar leaders, business people, sales people, ministers, educators and customer service representatives for some time. This book is released on the heels of the audio cassette version and both have been a labor of love. It is my hope that you find them valuable additions to your resource library, but more importantly, that you actually apply these principles to your daily life.

As humans, we are creatures of habit, and most of us have established some habits we are not proud of, nor are happy about. One of the wonderful things about life is that any learned behavior can be unlearned. Any principle that can be taught can be learned. Any habit we have can be replaced with a new habit. For most of us, this is not always easy. We want to be fit, but we have little time to go to the gym. We want to eat healthier, but who has time to cook? Besides, a burger with everything tastes better than a tofu salad- to me, anyway.

Our presentation skills are also habits. Have you ever noticed why some people continue to improve, while others stay the same for years? Why is that? Well, I have been a public speaker and educator for many years and have made communication a life-long study. I don't know all the answers, but I did find a few along the way. First, I found out that our success in life is directly proportional to our ability to communicate effectively. We have tremendous resources for better communication available to us, for a fraction of what it costs us in missed business opportunities and damaged or failed relationships. Isn't it ironic that with all that help the number one fear in the world is still public speaking? As Jim Rohn says "The guy's busy, I guess."

You are different of course, since you are reading this book. Some of these principles have been known for years. Many were born out of my classes and seminars as I searched for new ways to help people improve their communication skills and raise their level of self-confidence. As you apply the principles in this book, keep a journal to record your progress. Let me know how you are doing. You will feel better about your communication skills in a very short time. May God bless you and I hope we meet in the future.

Dedicated to the greatest secret of all, your power to love, have fabulous communication skills and willingly help others.

For my wife, Elaine, my Mom and my family, who always teach me to communicate with love.

Twelve Secrets Of A Great Voice

Acknowledgments-

I wish to acknowledge and thank so many people who helped make this book possible. First, I thank God for giving me the talent, knowledge and resources to make this project become a reality. I thank my wife, Elaine, for her love, encouragement, patience and late night editing. I thank my Mother for her unconditional love and total belief in my abilities. I thank Dads Henry and Paul, Jeanne and my sister Angela and her family for their encouragement and love. I thank my business partners, Pam DeLong and Michael Blain for their friendship and belief in the entrepreneurial dream and Ashish Shah for his friendship and efforts on the Web Site and the international market.

Thanks go to John Childress, Kristen Green and Patti McGee for their brilliant graphic creations, patience and support and Boyd Wade and Don Bourland for their invaluable business advice. Thanks also go to many people in Toastmasters International, American Seminar Leaders Association, National Speakers Association, American Society for Training and Development, National Storytelling Association, the University of Alaska-Anchorage-Adak and The University of Memphis. Thanks to all the students and seminar participants-you are wonderful.

Finally, I thank Jack VanBurg, Jeannie Terry, Harriet Diamond, Les Brown, Brian Tracy, Dana LaMon, Jimmy Grubbs, Anne Maddox, Cheryl Mims, Anne Peeples, Laura Moore, Jim Dawson, John Beavin, Claude Payton, F. J. Beverley, Myra Quick, Cindy Tipton, Rickey White, Tom Rieman, Dick Benson, David Stolzle, Lynn Pafford, Pauline Shirley, Jon Hornyak, Art Langlois and Captain Rever for their wonderful encouragement, guidance and belief in me.

Table of Contents

Twelve Secrets Of A Great Voice

Chapter One

Developing A New Way Of Speaking

Do you like the sound of your voice? Are there particular aspects of your voice that you would like to change? You are about to learn the Twelve Secrets that will help change the way you speak. No longer will you be ashamed of the sound of your voice. Recently, 78% of people polled said they did not like their voice. Public speaking ranks as the number one fear in the world. I suspect that it has a lot to do with the person's dissatisfaction about their voice. The rest has to do with staring out at all those eyeballs and faces and feeling inadequate when stepping up in front of a group. Don't think of your audience as naked, either, as some well meaning but misguided people will tell you to do. This will either gross you out or turn you on, neither of which is beneficial if you are about to give a major presentation.

You probably are making presentations in one or more ways; as part of your job, as a professional speaker, seminar leader or member of a Toastmasters International Club. I applaud you. Few things are as gratifying as giving effective presentations and being well received. While there are many interesting topics to speak on, a monotone, whiny, raspy, foghorn, or faint voice may be distracting or irritating your audience and minimizing your effectiveness. By contrast, a pleasant voice charms an audience. Getting command of your voice is a key step to success in your presentations, your career and your life.

My goal in writing this book is to help you get, and stay in the upper 22% of people who like the way they sound. We use our voices in business meetings, classrooms, on the phone, in conversations and on the stage. Mimes are the exception to this rule. When you apply these Twelve Secrets of improving your voice, you will start to do things that may be out of your current comfort zone. Keep applying the skills that you will develop and you will have no regrets. Many people live their whole lives in regret and frustration because they do not master the communication skills necessary to move up in business and develop personal relationships.

Therefore, they watch others pass them by in promotions and earning power. I like the teachings of Brian Tracy, who has come from relative obscurity to become a powerful figure in the field of communications today. Brian says "Do the thing you fear and the death of fear will surely come." This is so true. The more you work on these skills, the easier it becomes, the better *you* become and the more you increase your self-confidence. It's a simple formula that works every time!

You have made an excellent choice of skills to develop. Remember, **_you_** *are* the message, not all the technical toys that we have at our disposal today, such as multi-media computer presentation devices, overhead projectors, slide shows, laser pointers and dogs and ponies. Those are material things that are nice to have, but they can easily become crutches if we're not careful.

Since **_you_** *are* the message, let's look at the three things that help you make a first impression.

Appearance - How you look, grooming, facial expressions, body language.

Voice - Includes tonality, projection, melody, articulation, enunciation, regional and gender characteristics and delivery style, to name a few.

Content - Includes topics, grammar, sentence structure, and word selection. This also includes reactive responses. If you doubt this, get into a romantic relationship and report your findings to me in a month.

See how important your voice is in daily life? Many years ago, industry knowledge or technical expertise was just enough to be effective. Things have changed. Upper management expects everyone to express themselves when called upon to make a presentation. Developing your speaking voice will ensure that you're ready to speak up when it is your turn!

Socrates, Ciscero, Alexander the Great, Abraham Lincoln, Winston Churchill, Teddy Roosevelt, John F. Kennedy, Martin Luther King, Jr. , and Ronald Reagan were all great communicators. How? By combining a great voice with a powerful message to convey ideals that were bigger than themselves. We have the same opportunity with the power of our voice! You may not aspire to be a national or international figure, but *you can make a difference* in your life and the lives of many others, including your family. Is that ***exciting*** or what?!

Who are some of the present day figures you admire? For national broadcasters, names like; Tom Brokaw, Diane Sawyer, Lynn Russell, David Goodnow and political figures like; Elizabeth Dole and President Bill Clinton are often cited in my voice classes. I am sure you can think of others. Think of them now and list at least three qualities that you find in these or other people whom you admire for their speaking abilities or voice quality.

Name   _____   Quality I admire

_____

Name   _____   Quality I admire

_____

Name   _____   Quality I admire

_____

Some people say that knowledge is power. This is only half true. **Knowledge *put into action* is power.** So I am going to give you *Action Assignments* throughout this book to help you reach your goals. To bring your voice closer to the one you desire, do the following self-analysis to determine your abilities and goals. Then continue reading.

One of the most common letters dropped in everyday presentation and conversation is the "g" on "ing" ending words. We need to be aware of this pattern, as well as the tendency to diminish suffixes, yet another characteristic that is prevalent in communication today.

Having these good characteristics in your voice is very important. Another area we will spend more time on is *projection.* This is a process that broadcasters and business people and speakers constantly strive to improve. This secret is discussed at length in Chapter Seven.

These secrets will help you win over an audience each time you speak. As you listen to your recordings in the Action Assignments, compare them with the way you used to talk and the way other people talk.

There are several ways that people speak. To review just a few, some people speak in a monotone voice, while others speak with a lot of melody.

Some speak with a very weak voice, while others speak with a **very loud voice!** Some speak in the back of their throat and some speak in the *front,* which we call *fronting.*

Since *fronting* is an essential Secret that complements the other eleven Secrets, we will begin our first *Action Assignment* here. This will include a brief self-analysis questionnaire to help you improve immediately. Take your time in working through the *Action Assignments* to fully benefit from them. Mark the dates you actually do each exercise and refer frequently to your notes to measure your progress.

Action Assignment -

First, find an upbeat column from your local newspaper, usually in the lifestyle, travel or sports section. Pre-read the article to determine where the pauses are and read it into a tape recorder. Do not use your answering machine or a micro-cassette recorder as your primary recording system. They will not produce a high quality sound. Get a high quality audio system that will last a long time. If you have a stereo rack system, the duel cassette player is suitable. Most of these systems have a microphone and headphone jack. Go to your local electronics store and purchase a microphone, stand and headphones if you do not already have them. Also, use Maxell, TDK, or Sony 60 or 90 minute cassette tapes. Learning these Twelve Secrets on high quality sound equipment make a big difference.

Once you get the equipment, ask yourself the following questions and record the answers both on tape and in this journal section of the book. You may continue any answers in the pages provided at the back of this book. Remember to state or write the date when you work on these Action Assignments. This will help you review later.

Here are the questions:

1. Do I like the sound of my voice? _____ Why?

   _____

   _____

2. What are some of the things I like about my voice?

   _____

   _____

3. What are some of the things I dislike about my voice?

   _____

   _____

4. What are my current abilities as a speaker? The choices are: novice, experienced, very experienced, or professional [someone who speaks for fees.] ? _____

   _____

5. What goals do I want to accomplish with this book? Take plenty of time to list them. Then rank them in order of importance, with a deadline, i.e. end monotone-1 month.)

_____

_____

_____

_____

_____

_____

_____

_____

_____

Next, record three phone conversations (your side only), listen to them and circle the answers below that best describe your voice:

1. My Voice sounds: (a) monotone (b) squeaky (c) raspy (d) melodic.

2. I use: (a) too high of a pitch (b) too low of a pitch (c) the correct tonality

3. Do I: (a) lack vocal power (b) have too much power (c) know about vocal power?

4. Do I: (a) use a lot of filler words (um, you know, o.k.) (b) talk without fillers?

5. Do I: (a) run my sentences together (b) speak in clear sentences, using pauses?

6. Do I: (a) talk too soft (b) talk too loud (c) fluctuate my volume when speaking?

7. Do I: (a) mumble (b) bumble (c) stumble (d) ramble (e) rumble (f) speak clearly?

8. Do I: (a) sound mad (b) sad (c) disinterested (d) interested (e) interested (f) cheerful?

9. Do I: (a) fail to get the attention of my listener(s) (b) grab their attention?

10. Do I: (a) talk too slow (b) talk too fast (c) talk at a comprehensible rate?

11. Do I: (a) fail to identify myself (b) identify myself when I begin a call?

12. Do I: (a) smack gum, munch and crunch food or slurp a drink (b) wait until lunch?

13. Do I: (a) do other things while halfway listening (b) ask questions and listen intently?

14. Do I: (a) finish other people's sentences and/or cut them off (b) wait my turn?

15. Do I: (a) start and stop sentences (b) think before opening my mouth?

16. Do I: (a) lose my temper and take it out on someone (b) maintain control?

17. Do I: (a) cast a weak image (b) speak with authority?

18. Do I: (a) use slang, profanity and poor grammar (b) speak intelligently?

19. Do I: (a) have a regional or gender characteristic that labels me (b) sound neutral?

20. Do I: (a) use bland, trite words and phrases (b) use vivid imagery to paint pictures?

So, how did you rate yourself? If you scored higher in (b) or above, improvement will be easier. If you scored higher the (a) category, you just have to work a little harder. The grand news is that you will be able to improve immediately!

Remember, there are **Four Key Areas** to developing a great voice. They are:
1. Awareness 2. Coaching 3. Practice 4. Application.

You will be working in these Four Key Areas throughout this book. At first the changes will be hard to hear. After you develop new habits in approximately two weeks, you should start noticing some significant improvements. People at work, home, church, civic and social clubs will tell you about improvements in your voice too. These comments will confirm that you are developing a **GREAT VOICE!**

*In Chapter Two you will learn the **Secret of the Middle Third!***

Chapter One Notes

Chapter One Notes

_____

_____

_____

_____

_____

_____

_____

_____

_____

_____

_____

_____

_____

_____

Chapter Two

Discovering The Secret Of The Middle Third

Do you ever find yourself saying "There is *something* about that person I really like" as someone makes a presentation? We rarely say that about a person who has an annoying voice. The voice has to be pleasant sounding to get such favorable comments. Finding your **Middle Third** and developing a better image will have people saying that about *you*. Your listeners will sit up and take notice when you speak- on the stage, at work, in civic groups, at church and at social gatherings.

How is your middle? **Middle Third**, that is, not your midriff. This is about the natural tonality of your voice. In my classes and seminars, I find that few people are speaking with much richness in their voices. Ladies often sound strained, whiny, nasally or faint, while men sound low, gruff or gravely. Both sexes sound monotone a lot. Any combination of these characteristics is limiting your effectiveness as a speaker. How do we change? One of the first keys is to find your Middle Third.

	Upper Third
	MIDDLE THIRD
	Lower Third

Tonality Range Diagram

The diagram illustrates the three levels of voice tonality. They are: **the Upper Third**, the **Middle Third** and the **Lower Third**. Most people speak primarily in one of these tonality ranges. Many young women, especially receptionists (when you can find a live one), have squeaky voices, which makes them sound like a twelve year-old girl rather than the twenty-something women they really are. Have you heard them? They are too high-in the Upper Third. By contrast, some men could compete in a Henry Kissinger sound alike contest, with a very deep gravely, monotone, baritone sound that is almost as if a recording was playing in slow motion. They are too low-in the Lower Third.

Combining either of these sounds with a dry topic and poor presentation skills make listeners uneasy. They check their pagers and cell phones to see if they are working properly. (Would someone please page or call me so I can escape this torture?!) Maybe they will page themselves with their cell phone, tune out the speaker, whisper to their friends or just go to sleep! You will keep their attention with the sound of your voice!

The **Middle Third** is the best sound your voice can produce. Why? Because it has the richness we enjoy hearing in a person's voice. Successful singers, broadcasters and performers use this Middle Third to be more effective. Follow the guidelines in this chapter and you will be speaking with a combination of the Middle Third and Upper or Lower Third. My goal is to help you recognize and use your correct tonality (the Middle Third), and improve your presentations, both in person and on the phone.

Where is the Middle Third? Work with me now to find it. Slightly close your mouth so that your lips are barely touching. As I pose these questions to you, rather than affirming them with a "yes," I want you to just say "Um-humm," and do this in different pitches until your lips really buzz. We want buzzy lips here. Are you ready? Here we go. (1) Are you holding a book on developing your speaking voice? (2) Do you have opportunities to speak at work, civic clubs, church or social gatherings? (3) Does the sound of your voice bother you? (4) Are you determined to change your voice? (5) Have you ever smiled at an attractive person? (6) Do you feel your lips buzzing?

Keep doing this until you feel your lips buzz. When this happens, you have found your **Middle Third**! Congratulations! This is your natural voice, hidden by years of incorrect speaking. When you get the Secret of the **Middle Third**, you will not be speaking too high or too low. You will speak in a natural tone every time you make a presentation or hold a casual conversation. Your Middle Third is where you will get the most projection, tonality and other sound qualities of your voice. The Upper and Lower Thirds will help to provide a rich sounding voice. However, the strongest tonality comes from staying in the Middle Third.

The best time to do this buzzy lips "um-humm" exercise is when you first awake. Why? This is because your vocal folds have had a chance to relax during sleep. As you go through your morning bathroom rituals, this is a quick and simple technique to find the right tonality. Also, the sound you hear as you first speak after a long rest period is your natural Middle Third sound. For instance, have you ever had an early morning phone call after you have been up less than thirty minutes? The sound of your voice during that call is the perfect example of the Middle Third.

Try this as an exercise. Make an early morning telephone call and record your side of the conversation. Whom do you call in the early morning? That's up to you. Call the local radio station and try to be caller number five. Call the local school to ask questions about upcoming basketball, football, baseball games or track events (even if you do not have kids in school there). How do they know? Call your sister in Albuquerque and say 'Hi.' Call your Aunt Ruby in Rhode Island and ask about her gall bladder operation. Call your mother and tell her you love her. That will make her day.

You can do this quick tonality check at work by simply answering an affirmative question with "um-humm" instead of "yeah, uh-huh" or other common answers. When you feel your lips buzz or tingle, you will *know* what is happening. Condition your voice to be in that middle range and adjust your hearing to recognize the tonality. Another quick way to check for tonality correctness is to put two fingers on the side of your throat while saying "um-humm" in different tones, both up and down the melodic scale.

The strong buzzing feel will be very evident to your fingers when you find the Middle Third. Try this now. It might take a little effort at first, but you can feel it. Have some fun with this, trying to go in the

Upper Third, then in the Lower Third. When you go to the extremes of highs and lows you do not feel the buzzing, do you? That is the reason it is so important to find your Middle Third. When you start speaking with the Middle Third, people are going to comment to you and others that they like your voice!

Now let's review the physical composition that contributes to our speaking voice. First, we have the *larynx*, or voice box, which is just a short passageway the connects the pharynx to the trachea. It lies in the neck anterior, or in front of the throat, to the fourth or sixth cervical vertebrae. The walls of the larynx are supported by nine pieces of carti-lage. The Adam's Apple, or *thyroid* consists of two fused plates that form the anterior wall of the larynx and give it the triangular shape we notice in boys and men. Although both sexes have them, this thyroid cartilage is much bigger in males than females. The larynx is built in two folds, an upper pair, which is called the ventricular folds, or false vocal cords, and the lower pair, which is called the true vocal cords.

The air passageway between the walls of these two sections is called the *glottis*. Your pitch is controlled by tension placed on the true vocal cords. If air passes against the vocal folds, they vibrate and send up sound waves in a column of air through the nose, mouth and pharynx. The sound becomes louder as air pressure increases. Let's review how that happens. The skeletal muscles of the larynx, which are called the intrinsic muscles, are attached internally to the pieces of ridged cartilage and to the vocal folds themselves. Each time the muscles contract, the ligaments (cords), are pulled tight and are stretched out into the air pas-sageway, thus making the glottis narrow. If the cords are pulled taught by the muscles, they vibrate more rapidly, resulting in a higher pitch. Lower sounds are produces by decreasing the tension on the cords.

The vocal cords are usually longer and thicker in males than in females and vibrate more slowly. (This is why men generally have a lower range of pitch than women.) Sound originates from the vibration of the true vocal cords. However, other physical components are necessary for converting the sound into recognizable speech. They include the phar-ynx, mouth and nasal cavity. These and the para-nasal sinuses act as reso-nating chambers to give each person's voice their distict human and indi vidual characteristics.

By constricting and relaxing the muscles in the walls of the pharynx, we produce the vowel sounds (A, E, I, O, U). Also, muscles of the face, tongue and lips help us to enunciate our words. When someone experiences laryngitis, it results from an inflammation of the larynx, which is often caused by a respiratory infection or irritants, such as cigarette smoke. Inflammation of the vocal cords themselves cause hoarseness or loss of the voice by interfering with the contraction of the cords, or by causing them to swell to the point where they cannot vibrate freely. Many long-term smokers acquire a permanent hoarseness and cough from the damage done by chronic inflammation. So, smokers beware. You are damaging your vocal system when you smoke. I used to smoke, but gave it up when I started having trouble breathing. With help and encouragement from people around you, you can give it up too. Please do this for your family.

Next is the trachea. The trachea, or windpipe is the tubular passage for air, about 12 centimeters, or 4-1/2 inches in length and 2.5 centimeters, or 1 inch in diameter. It is located in the front of the esophagus and extends from the larynx to the fifth thoracic vertebra, where it divides into right and left primary bronchi. The trachea plays a significant part in our speaking, since it helps deliver air from the lungs. The trachea then terminates into the chest by dividing into a right primary bronchus (which goes to the right lung) and a left primary bronchus (which goes into the left lung). The right primary bronchus is more vertical, shorter and wider than the left primary bronchus. As a result, foreign objects that enter the passageway frequently lodge in that area. Like the trachea, the primary bronchi contain incomplete rings of cartilage and are lined with substance to help keep the passageway free.

The bronchi are attached to the lungs, which are paired, cone-shaped organs and are lying in the thoracic cavity, which is your chest area. They are separated from each other by the heart and other structures in the mediastinum. In 1987 I had a surgical operation to remove a tumor in this area. The surgeons referred to the tumor as a mediastinal mass and the surgical procedure is known as a thoracotomy. The surgeons had to collapse my right lung to perform the operation. When you are given the choice to leave the mass in or have an operation near your heart, you appreciate having good health and being with your family and friends. Now back to biology class.

Two layers of cirrus membrane (collectively called the plural membrane), enclose and protect each lung. The outer layer is attached to the walls of the plural cavity and is called the perithial pleura. There is fluid that prevents friction between the membrane. When the inflammation of the plural membrane exists, it is a condition called pleurisy. You may have experienced this or know someone who has had this condition. The inflammation causes friction during breathing, which could be quite painful when the swollen membranes rub against each other. With today's advanced medical technology, we have relief for this condition, thus preventing long term suffering and a weakened voice.

The lungs extend from the diaphragm to a point just above the clavicle and lie against the ribs in the front and the back. The diaphragm, or bread basket, helps get the air down into the lungs for the breathing cycle. The right lung is thicker and broader than the left lung. It also is shorter than the left lung because the diaphragm is higher on the right side to accommodate the liver that lies below it. The left lung is thinner, narrower and longer than the right lung. Did you know that?

Let's move on to breathing and lung capacity. Breathing in is called 'inspiration' or 'inhalation.' Just before each inhalation, the air pressure inside the lungs equals the pressure of the atmosphere, which is about 760mm hg at standard conditions. The first step towards increasing the lung volume, (extremely important to developing a great voice), involves contraction of the respiratory muscles or the diaphragm and the external muscles. The diaphragm is the sheet of skeletal muscle that forms the floor of the thoracic cavity. As it contracts, it moves downward, thereby increasing the depth of the thoracic cavity. Just like blinking, our breathing cycle is done subconsciously.

Here's Your Action Assignment-

Let's do the bread basket push again. Put your hand together flat against the lower part of your breastplate (think brassiere zone), fingers touching. Take a deep breath, hold your mouth almost closed and exhale while pushing slightly on your breadbasket. Please do this now. Do not skip over this part thinking you'll do it later. Let the air out slowly and easily to maximize the time you can do the exercise. You can get a partner or group of friends to time each person to see who can exhale the longest. Your goal is to increase your lung capacity until you can sustain the exhaling process to at least 45-60 seconds. With a little practice you can probably last 90 seconds. If you are a runner (like me), you should easily last 60 seconds in the beginning. This exercise will also help you to gain more endurance for all kinds of physical activity. Hubba Hubba.

We have a tremendous capacity for air in our lungs and an ability to increase our diaphragmatic breathing. Get into the habit of doing this exercise five to ten times every day (five to ten minutes). It will increase your breathing, improve your whole biological system and help you project your voice naturally without straining to be heard. You will no longer need to rely on public address systems to reach all members of your audience. Whether you are at a Toastmasters function, PTA meeting, church setting, business meeting or speaking professionally at a banquet or seminar, your rich voice using the Middle Third will be carried farther by extended breathing.

Areas that help you develop that Middle Third sound include; the *glottis,* which is the bottom area, the *vocal folds,* and the *ventricular folds* (which are just above the *vocal folds). The epiglottis* and *base of the tongue* complete the system. The entire area is always working to help you develop that natural sound, using the Middle Third. Your knowledge of what is happening in your breathing system will remind you to project your voice with a rich tonality.

Let's review the tonality scale. If you have any musical knowledge at all, you will recognize this scale. If not, that's O.K. Using a piano, the idea of tonality and the melodic scale is easy to follow. If you do not have access to one, go to a piano store and ask a salesperson to show you how it works. (Feel free to take this book with you.) Each key on the piano is a note. The musical scale is: A>B>C>D>E>F>G>A B>C>D>E>F>G>A>B>C>D>E>F>G>A>B>C>D>E>F>G. You get the idea. There are minor notes too, but we will just concentrate on the majors for simplicity. Your task is to understand how this concept applies to your voice. As you go up or down the scale, you are creating a melody. That's all music is, a series of melodic notes, strung together like a chain. Since I am a musician (guitar, banjo and piano), I listen to songs on a recording and learn to play them. Like songs, your Middle Third is in a certain key.

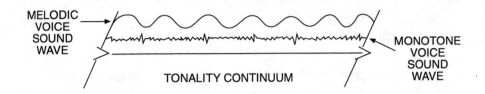

The Tonality Continuum graphically represents the sound of monotone and melodic sound waves. You can see how the monotone sound
wave remains very low and flat while the melodic sound wave has peaks
and valleys, much like a song uses the musical scale. Your goal is to
sound more like the melodic sound wave.

Practice your Middle Third exercise right now and match it with a
note on the musical scale. If you want to do this at home on a low budget,
go to a music store and ask for a pitch pipe. They cost about $5.00.
Another inexpensive but great practice instrument is a guitar. You can
find them in music stores, the classified ads, garage sales and even in
pawn shops for less than $100. I recommend taking someone with you
who knows a little about guitars so you will get a fair deal. Acoustic
guitars are great starters, because you may really want to learn how to
play well. I've been a musician for about sixteen years. It is fun and very
rewarding. Find a friend who will show you the scale and all the major
chords (A-G). If you do not know anyone personally, take a few lessons
at a local music store that sells guitars. If you have a piano, use it.

Get yourself comfortable to practice. Whatever instrument you
have chosen, slowly match each note on the scale with your voice. Don't
read this and say 'I can't sing, carry a tune in a bucket' or other self-
defeating thoughts. Some teacher, a parent or other adult may have told
you this when you were young. Except in extremely rare cases, this is
shear nonsense. You can do the most remarkable things. You just have to
make up your mind that you *will not* be limited by what someone else has
said about your abilities, or lack thereof. Practice this exercise and dis-
cover that you are *not* tone deaf!

Try to match higher and lower notes as you read a magazine,
newspaper or book aloud. You will see how hard it is to speak in a wide

range for long periods of time. That's because your voice generally uses very flat monotones, until you learn about melody. Over the first two weeks of working on this Secret, I want you to stay focused on the sound of your natural Middle Third voice and the melody that you hear. Record this sound and play it back over and over for several days to hear how you truly can sound your best. Why? Your ears have heard the *old* you for a long time. We are training them to hear the *new* you. Follow these instructions and you will improve your voice much quicker.

Another helpful habit to sustain the voice is to sip a glass of orange juice as you record yourself reading aloud in the morning. Take heart caffeine fans! You can also drink coffee. However, sipping a glass of orange juice helps build your vocal cords and prevents hoarseness throughout the day. This is the equivalent of giving your car a tune up and oil change before entering the Indy 500. If you do not or cannot drink orange juice, pick a juice that contains Vitamin C. Just establish the habit of drinking juice every morning. This helps your vocal cords and the rest of your body feel energetic rather than exhausted throughout the day. If you have any doubts or cannot get away from having that Coke and Twinkie for breakfast, try this for thirty days. Then you can assume your current morning habits.

To summarize this chapter, the Secret of the Middle Third will help you develop richness and tonality variation in your voice. Obviously, our physical composition plays a vital role in how we sound, yet many people choose to live in poor health by having poor health habits. When you have good health and richness in tonality, your voice can be a lightning rod for listeners to receive your message. Finding your Middle Third is one of the first keys to successful speaking.

Now that you know the Secret of the Middle Third, you are on your way to developing a **GREAT VOICE!!**

In Chapter Three we will discuss the *Secret of Increasing Your Vocal Vitality!*

Chapter Two Notes

_____

_____

_____

_____

_____

_____

_____

_____

_____

_____

_____

_____

_____

Chapter Two Notes

_____

_____

_____

_____

_____

_____

_____

_____

_____

_____

_____

_____

_____

Chapter Three

Increasing Your Vocal Vitality

Would you like to set yourself apart from the crowd? With this Secret of *energizing* your voice, you will improve your presentations in person and on the telephone. In this chapter we will also review easy relaxation techniques to start the day, prepare for a presentation and avoid laryngitis.

You only have one chance to make a first impression and the basic three elements of a first impression are within your control. They are: (1) **Your appearance-** people are going to take a look at you to determine your credibility. (2) **Your voice-** how you sound gives the listener a certain image of you, especially on the telephone. Your voice is a calling card; it announces to the world who you are what degree of self confidence you have. Vocal vitality is key to conveying that image. (3) **Your message-** the thoughts, ideas, words and emotions you share with your listeners, one-on-one or in groups. All three elements make a lasting impression on your audience. We all want to make a favorable impression on our listeners, especially if we are giving presentations in business or civic settings.

For instance, if you spoke at a banquet and looked like a bum, you would definitely make an impression. Maybe not a favorable one, but you would get their attention. If you looked like a movie star, but your voice sounded as if you were a young child or a record played at slow speed, you would make a certain impression. If you looked great and your voice was pleasant, but you talked in vague circles or used profanity, you would make a different impression. These are just a few of the possible scenarios that are incredibly real in the world of pubic speaking and corporate meetings. This is why it is so important to work on vocal variety and vitality. Speakers who energize their voices impact their audiences favorably throughout the entire presentation.

The Secret of increasing your vocal vitality is easy to implement if you have the determination and discipline to practice these techniques. Keep the rewards of better communication and higher self-confidence in mind and you won't have any problems accomplishing the goals in this chapter.

The first thing that I want you to do is analyze the people you see making presentations. Go beyond their message and study their voice and mannerisms. Next, look around the room to see the expressions (or lack thereof), on the faces of the audience. Are they listening intently and smiling or laughing when appropriate. Are they fidgeting and whispering or do they have that 'deer in the headlights' look? This quick analysis will tell you a lot about how a speaker's voice and mannerisms affect an audience.

When I started focusing on this aspect of public speaking, I realized how much *power* the voice has in effective communication. I have seen numerous speakers get up with a great topic, only to bore the audience to death! I have also seen very nervous speakers ruin their presentations with a monotone voice or use of excessive filler words. Some, but not all, include: um, ah, er, you know, O.K., etc. If you are a beginning speaker, this book will help you break those habits before they discourage you forever. We will discuss how to eliminate fillers and a monotone voice more in Chapters Ten and Eleven.

If you are a minister, you have increased competition from other churches for members and endless secular activities for member involvement. Now, more than ever it is important to have vocal vitality when you address the congregation. A minister or lay leader who wakes up the congregation will have a growing church. This also applies to the entire ministry staff. You can make a great impact on people's lives with a strong message delivered with **vigor.** Read on to make an even greater impact by developing your speaking voice.

Another key area where vocal vitality is important is in telephone skills. How are your telephone skills? Does your voice convey your message with energy or lethargy? Many people have no idea how low energy their voice sounds on the phone. This is evident when you speak to many customer service representatives or call centers that process orders by phone. Have you found this to be true? If you haven't had much experience with this, try calling a catalog toll free number or a customer service center from a major retail store. If fact, call ten places and get some information or a catalog sent to you. Keep a record of the following characteristics. (1) Were they [a] friendly [b] tolerant [c] indifferent [d] rude? (2) Was their voice [a] pleasant [b] monotone [c] nasal [d] high or low? (3) Was their voice [a] energetic [b] average [c] low energy [d] faint and whispery?

You can also use this quick check list to rate yourself and others on the phone and in person. The analysis of other voices will help you improve your own voice quickly and easily. Most people do not realize how much voice improvement helps their image and self-confidence until they begin this process. With a little time and practice, you are going to master this skill!

Is vocal vitality important in today's hectic business world? Yes. Vitality is something that is quite lacking in most telephone business conferences that I have experienced. Many times the other person is not communicating with any kind of energy or enthusiasm in their voice. It's sort of like when someone shakes your hand and you expect a firm grip and get a cold fish feeling from them instead. That comes through in your voice, too. Haven't you ever talked with someone that lacks energy, enthusiasm, vitality or anything? They act as they are auditioning for a zombie movie. Conversely, when someone grips your hand with warmth, excitement and energy, or speaks in a very energetic manner, you get that positive message as well. Your voice communicates your positive or negative attitude to everyone you meet.

How did you develop your current way of speaking? Part of it is feeling free to be who you are. We cannot all talk like John Wayne or Diane Sawyer. As you build your self-confidence, you will learn how to express yourself more freely and vocally.

There are four key elements in a great voice. They are:

(1) **VOLUME** - Some people can easily raise the volume of their voices. My football coach in high school had tremendous volume. He yelled at us day and night, with and without a megaphone. Loud volume is a common characteristic of men. Granted, there are some women that could make you stand at attention, but they are few in numbers. The men who speak loudly annoy the audience when they begin booming in an average room. Heaven help you if you find yourself next to them in a cubical or seated next to them at a social function.

Most loud people do not realize they are so loud. Please help this type of person before he or she makes another presentation by pulling them aside and tell them gently. They will thank you for it later and so will your other co-workers and friends.

The other extreme is a person who is too soft spoken. They are barely audible in an elevator. Often they don't feel like leading a group in silent prayer. Speaking up in meetings is out of the question. Their peers may not take them seriously, which adversely affects their self-confidence. Picture this scenario. You are a shy, quiet, soft spoken person just about to share your insights with the staff, and Mr. Big Mouth steps in and tells everyone, 'What Susan is trying to say is ....' Results? You never get another word in edgewise. Have you ever seen this happen? Has this ever happened to you? If you do not have the vocal vitality to hold your audience's attention, it may be holding you back from higher earnings. Now is the time to address it and become **bold!** *You can do it!*

Conduct an analysis. The next time you see someone speaking with a very soft tone of voice, notice the faces of the audience. Are they focusing intently on the speaker? They are looking around the room, looking at their watches, playing with their tapioca, doodling, or any number of things that could occupy their minds. Also, conduct an analysis of a speaker who has vocal vitality and energy in their voice. Notice the faces of the audience. What are they doing? Chances are great they will be nodding in agreement on most key points, smiling or laughing when appropriate and listening intently for what is coming next. **That's very powerful.** The speaker is effective because he or she has the audience's attention throughout the entire presentation. You will too, by the end of this chapter. Remember, the more animated you are with your voice and gestures, the more your audience will be giving you their full attention. It happens every time.

Conduct another analysis. Record yourself reading a section of the newspaper first, then giving a presentation. How do you sound? Are you soft, loud, average or exceptional? Rate yourself honestly and work to bring your voice up to *exceptional*. Be sure to get close enough to the microphone to adequately pick up your voice. Sometimes my students set the recorder in the back of the room. This renders their voice barely audible. Please don't do this. Lapel mikes work best and you can pick them up at Radio Shack or most electronics stores. Call around your area and find out if there are any special sales in progress. Merchandise is always being upgraded and clearance sales are common. See appendix for more details.

(2) **RATE** - The rate at which we speak is incredibly important. Your rate of delivery originated from mimicking your parents, relatives, teachers and friends. Some regional rates and dialects are directly proportional to the lifestyle in that part of the world. In the Northeastern United States, around New York and New Jersey, people tend to speak a lot faster than in the Deep South. Why? Because the pace is fast, fast, fast, everything is hurry up, get it done faster, the population is higher and the culture is impatient. In the Southeast, also called the Deep South, agriculture is still the major industry. The pace is slower, the population is lower per capita and the people tend to have a Mountain Dew, Coke or iced tea while conducting business or a casual conversation.

My friend, Boyd Wade once said that the difference in living in Memphis and living in Alabama is that in Memphis, things are slow, but in Alabama they have come to a grinding halt. He went to the University of Alabama-Birmingham on a four year scholarship. It took him five years to get his degree. He said he drove down there in five hours. It took him eight hours to get back.

In speaking, the appropriate rate of speed varies with your location. For some regional and international cultures, speaking rapidly is common. The average rate of speed is 120-160 words per minute. Speak at a rate that engages your audience but also helps you stay on track. Too fast of a delivery will lose your audience quickly. Some technical people tend to rush through the information, slides blazing, using acronyms from beginning to end. Results? Everyone is baffled. Then they say "Are there any questions?" No one raises their hand. Please don't let this be you. Your vocal vitality can be such a <u>valuable</u> tool to getting your ideas across effectively. Record yourself during a presentation and count the words per minute. Also, listen for places that you sounded rushed. Chances are very good that you diminished a few suffixes and/or ran sentences together. See Chapters Nine and Ten to handle these issues.

If you speak English as a second language, I admire you, and ask that you please slow your rate of speed when speaking English. I have been very fortunate to live in many historic and exotic places in the world, including four different islands. (That's another book.) One thing that impresses me about people from other countries is that they are very willing to learn something new. If you are reading this book and English is a second language, please practice pronouncing each word distinctly. I train people from six different countries and this is where I begin to help everyone improve. In Session Ten of the Twelve Secrets Audio series I give you assignments to build your vocabulary. You will hear improvement in no time at all!

Always try to hear and see you presentation from the audience's point of view. They are trying to digest your message and will appreciate anything you do to make this an easy task for them.

(3) **PITCH -** This is a common vocal characteristic that many people do not like about themselves. If you have too high or too low of a pitch, it's distracting to your listeners as you speak. This area was covered in Chapter Two on the Secret of the Middle Third. It's so important to find your Middle Third and stay there. Many people have stayed in the incorrect speaking zone for years. If you are one of these people, now is the time to change, without surgery or years of clinical therapy. Please go back to Chapter Two, review your Action Assignments to develop your Middle Third and use the correct pitch!

(4) **QUALITY -** Your voice should have a rich sound quality. When you learn to relax your voice and speak without straining it, you will begin to feel and hear the richness I am describing. People with rough voices, such as Redd Foxx, Joe Cocker and those that portray gangsters in the movies would probably test our patience if they were public speakers.

Why? We want to hear a more melodious sound during public presentations. A rich quality voice portrays friendliness and sincerity. How do you start? Study people.

Action Assignment-

Just take a little survey next week. Ask two to four friends to help you take a 'silent survey.' Purchase everyone an inexpensive, pocket size note pad. Each person will make a note of the number of people they see and hear present a topic in person. Of that number, check off how many actually speak as they are *excited* about the topic they are discussing. On the evening of the seventh day, get together over dinner and compile the information. Your survey results will probably be surprising to everyone involved. Next, each person gets a chance to reenact the presentation that was the *least* exciting. For a little fun and competition, have a prize for the best imitation and cast paper ballots to determine the winner. This will be a lot of laughs!

Then talk about why these presentations were so ineffective, with the emphasis on voice energizing and an analysis of how the person could increase his/her vocal vitality. Have someone serve as a facilitator and list your ideas on a flip chart or big note pad. This will serve to remind you of all the characteristics that you want to avoid! Who needs a TV or other entertainment when you have each other?! You can start forming groups by asking people in your Toastmasters Club, National Speakers Association Chapter or other interested parties.

Next, get some balloons. It's time to celebrate! Actually, I want you to get a big package of balloons and distribute one to each person. Blow them up to capacity. Keeping the balloon in your mouth, let the air out slowly. You will feel your cheeks fill as the air escapes from your mouth. Do this at least five times a day for two weeks to increase your lung capacity. Don't say 'This is a stupid idea-I'm not a kid anymore.' Is that right? Try this at least once. If you don't feel great and have fun with your friends, then pass the Grey Poupon and start a Dullpersons Club. I do this in my classes and seminars and people just love it! So what do you have to lose? Nothing! Get the kids in on this fun.

Lastly, record yourself exaggerating the verbs, adverbs and nouns in a newspaper or magazine article until this voice becomes your natural voice. Do this while in the kitchen while the dishwasher is running. You can also turn on the blender, mixer, range hood and vaccum cleaner. This helps you increase your vocal vitality by competing for volume with mechanical sounds rather than the TV noise. Get your kids or the neighbor's kids in on this to have more fun. Kids like to scream. Just ask them. After you do these Action Assignments for a few weeks, you will notice a big difference in the way people react to you when you speak because you will have *more **vocal vitality.***

This means that you are on your way to developing a **GREAT VOICE!!**

*In Chapter Four, we will discuss **Getting Control for More Self-Confidence!***

Chapter Three Notes

Chapter Three Notes

_____

_____

_____

_____

_____

_____

_____

_____

_____

_____

_____

_____

_____

Chapter Four

Getting Control for More Self-Confidence

You should be proud of your heritage. At the same time, in business, your regional characteristics could be limiting you in reaching diverse audiences. As I mentioned in Chapter Three, dialects are developed regionally. I do not intend to imply that any one region is superior to another. I'm saying that regional characteristics sometimes prevent business deals and friendships from forming. We *can* get control of regional and gender voice characteristics. It takes awareness, coaching, practice and discipline. You can accomplish your goals in this area if you are willing to do what it takes.

The first step in this process is taping yourself. By now you should have a nice tape recorder to do these practice assignments. Record yourself reading an article from a newspaper, magazine or favorite book. Compare your voice with the neutral sound of the national newscasters on Headline News, ABC, CBS, NBC or the Fox network. If you do not have cable, go to a friend's house or go to the electronics department of your friendly neighborhood Wal-Mart. If that's not available, go to Grandma's house. She will love you for thinking of her.

Through extensive research I have discovered why people accent words a certain way. Are you ready? You pronounce vowels a certain way, either by elongating the vowels — Do-or (such as in a Southern accent), or you compress the vowels -- Dor (Northwestern accent).

A consonant is a speech sound produced by occluding (p,b;t,d;k,g), diverting (m,n,ng), or obstructing (f,v;s,z,etc). It is also is the flow of air from the lungs (opposed to a vowel sound) -- a, e, i, o, u.

These sounds help you compose your words. If you have a heavy accent (and many people do), someone from your area may be able to understand you. However, someone who speaks with a different accent and vocabulary may have trouble listening and comprehending what you are saying. Communication is a two-way process. If we forget this, we may blame our audience for not understanding us. We <u>must</u> improve *our* communication skills if we plan to reach diverse audiences and become successful.

How can you improve your vowels and consonants? If you are elongating your vowels, strive to compress them. If you are compressing your vowels, elongate them. Elongated or compressed vowels will make it harder for your listeners to follow your presentation, unless they are from your region and speak like you. You must challenge yourself to expand your presentation opportunities beyond your current 'audience comfort zone.' Speaking to a room full of total strangers is very exhilarating! Diverse audiences are the best! You must rise to the challenge!

Let's review a few common words. Take the word 'DOOR.' If you elongate those two 'OO' s, they would almost form two syllables when the word is actually one syllable. Elongating the word makes it stretch like a rubber band along the horizontal plane.

Conversely, if you are a compressing type speaker and say the word 'COFFEE,' it may look like this: 'COUFE.' This indicates a sharp vowel sound. You can easily modify it by elongating it just a bit. Try saying 'CAUFAEE.' This is an exaggeration, but it will help you stretch your vowel sounds to become more neutral.

Pause here. Set up your tape recorder and record yourself saying:

1. DOOR   2. COFFEE   3. PARK

Listen for the sound of your vowel pronunciation and work to modify them to sound neutral. Read an article and pay attention to the sounds you are making with each word. You can also use your VCR to record a short segment of the national news. Listen to how the professional broadcasters sound. Play a short segment of the tape and record yourself repeating the news story. This will train your ears to recognize the neutral sounds of the vowels and consonants.

Find a short newspaper or magazine article and highlight or underline all words that start with the vowels: A, E, I, O, U. Read the article into the recorder and listen for the vowel pronunciations. Are you elongating, compressing or do you sound relatively neutral? Keep working on this and use a different tape for each week of practice. Remember to record the date during the taping session and on the label. These will become a valuable part of your audio library. They also will be great to measure how much progress you are making!

When we look at gender characteristics, we find that men tend to mumble, display a lack of energy, speak in a monotone voice and speak in the Lower Third (see Chapter Two). For ladies, the characteristics are: speaking in the Upper Third (Chapter Two), speaking too faintly and trailing off at the ends of sentences.

One of the best ways to learn how you are doing is to constantly tape yourself and play it back for review. There is no difference in the way you sound on tape and the way you sound to your listeners. Many people think they have a different voice on tape, but that's simply not true. There is one simple reason you hear it differently as you speak. You have bones in your head! That's why they called me 'Bonehead!' We all have them. They prevent us from hearing our voice as true as our listener does. I will say this many times in this book; to create a great voice we must be aware of all the factors that make up our communication skills. With this knowledge we can make adjustments, improve and become great communicators. Without it, we can remain average our whole lives. The choice is ours to make.

Action Assignment-

Record three phone conversations (your side only). Listen for the characteristics that we have reviewed in this chapter. You are now only focusing on the gender characteristics. Find an upbeat article in the newspaper and read it onto your practice tape. Modify each distracting habit one at a time until you have mastered it. Then move on to the next one. You will eventually replace the old habits with the new ones. Your progress should be very noticeable after two weeks. For some it will be quicker, for others may take a little longer. Stay with it and you will hear and see results!

In Summary-

Your voice is one of your most important assets. Your communication skills are all that you have to get you through life. When you start getting control of these regional and gender characteristics, you begin the building process to greater self-confidence. Why? You will feel like taking on bigger and better things. You will no longer be satisfied to sit back and watch the world go by. You will get in there and participate. Life is just like a football game. You are either on the field, on the bench or in the bleachers. Where are you now? Where do you want to be in one year, two years, five years and ten years from now? I am telling you from personal experience, including years of hard knocks and mediocrity, if you want to get ahead and get on the field, this is your chance to prepare for it. Getting control of your voice and pubic speaking skills will catapult you to the front of the crowd and on the field. Go for it. When you get Control of regional and gender characteristics, you are on your way to developing a *GREAT VOICE!*

YOU CAN DO IT!!

In Chapter Five we will discuss how you can *Speak With Authority At Work!*

Are you ready?

Chapter Five

Speaking With Authority At Work

In this chapter, we will look at speaking with increased vigor and emphasis to get your point across more effectively in meetings. Convincing your listeners of the value of your message is accomplished through several modes of communication.

The **first** key element is *your position* in the organization. If, for example, you are in a management position, or even a vice-presidential role, your listeners respect the *authority* of the position. The pecking order of the organization puts you in either an enviable position as the presenter, or in a slightly disadvantaged position, if many people in the group outrank you. We all know how some people really play this political game to their maximum advantage, sometimes at the expense of others. *This* Secret will give you a completely honest advantage in the group, no matter what position you hold. Think about it for a minute. There are a lot of high ranking people in organizations that can't lead a group in silent prayer! Why? It's because they need to improve their communication skills. This is where you now have a distinct advantage.

The **second** key element is the *message* itself. What content are you bringing to the presentation or discussion? Is it technical, general information or powerful knowledge that will benefit everyone in the room? Is the message; nice to know, need to know information or does the message have an impact on the bottom line of the organization? There is a difference in the way your listeners will respond to each sort of message. The technical presenter (I know, because I used to be an engineer in the Navy), may bring enough data to conduct a presentation for two weeks straight! If you are a technical person, do not give in to that temptation. Be informative, be brief and be seated.

A person who effectively speaks with authority (in this case it could technical expertise), constanly thinks of his or her audience when preparing and delivering a message. Most technical people only recite information and give little thought of the benefits to the listeners. A technical speaker's ability is enhanced if he or she focuses on what is important to the audience. If you will remember this, you will be far ahead of your peers. For non-technical types, your presentations will range from informative to persuasive to evoking emotion. Just remember the acronym **PIE**, which stands for **Persuasive, Informative** and **Emotional.** At least two of these styles are in most presentations, with one being more dominate than the other. Know your audience and use the appropriate style for them. For an effective message, do a quick analysis of the audience and tailor the message to them. It works every time. Try it.

The **third** key element to speaking with authority at work is *the inflection of your voice.* Many people who present as part of their job have no idea how to speak effectively. Speaking to them is like going to the bathroom. They do it, but only out of necessity. They speak in an even, monotonous delivery style where none of the words are emphasized. This makes it challenging for the listeners and they will tune out quickly. You want the listeners to be attentive to <u>you</u> and <u>your message</u> throughout the whole presentation.

How can you develop great vocal inflection? First, remember that all great sports broadcasters have the ability to speak with inflection as they report a sports story. You can verify this by watching and listening to a sports broadcaster on television or radio. Someone like John Madden, who is a professional football sportscaster for Fox TV, has really mastered this skill. Your local sportscasters can give you some examples of this technique on their newscasts as well. Tune in and focus on the way they deliver the information. Most well respected sportscasters have a sense of *excitement* when they speak! This is one of the key elements of your voice that you need to work on to gain more self-esteem and speak with authority. If *you* can't get excited about your subject, how do you expect your audience to get excited about it? Also, most employment ads state that the successful candidate must possess good oral and written communication skills. Where do you start?

Pick an article from the newspaper, preferably the sports section. Highlight or underline the key action verbs, nouns, pronouns and consonants. Read the article silently several times to mentally rehearse the way it will sound. Then read it aloud, **_emphasizing_** and **_exaggerating_** the highlighted words. Record it and play it back to listen for the way you sound. This will give you a sense of how much better you sound when putting life into your presentation.

Bosses often give speaking opportunities to an assistant. If you are in this category, take every opportunity at work, church and civic clubs to speak and see how your career leaps ahead at lightening speed. If you haven't already joined, become a member of Toastmasters International. Call 1-800-WE SPEAK (937-7325) or (714) 858-8255 to find out about clubs in your area. You can also write or call me at 1-800-989-2013 or (901) 755-2013 to find out more about this wonderful organization. I also suggest that you take a Dale Carnegie Course in Effective Communication and Human Relations. These classes are so valuable that you will change your life and never look back. I have been associated with both Toastmasters International and Dale Carnegie & Associates for several years. Nothing can compare to both programs for developing your self-confidence and speaking skills. Again, call me for more information. Later, after you have done several presentations successfully, your confidence and your abilities as a speaker will take you in directions you never dreamed of before. Then something wonderful will happen.

Imagine this scene. The president of the company comes up to you after a successful presentation and says "Linda, I really liked the way you communicated those ideas to the staff. Starting Monday, you'll be promoted to vice-president of this department and your office will be on the twentieth floor. Please see me later this afternoon to discuss your raise." *Are you with me!? Great! Read on.*

How can I sound enthusiastic when I don't lead an exciting life? Easy. Act enthusiastic when you speak!! Nobody wants to hear someone who sounds like one of those old record players with a crank that ran down after ten minutes of play. Yet, many people sound like that all the time, especially on the telephone. They have a flat, unexciting, non-authoritative sounding voice. If you have been doing this, NOW is the time to start using your new voice. You may not sound as impressive as the sportscaster on the eleven o'clock news at first, but at least you'll sound better than 95% of the people you hear in public every day. Think about it. You can be in the top 5%!

Using increasing emphasis and vigor as you read an underlined passage aloud will help you develop the habit of speaking like this normally. It may take a while, but if you do this at least once a day for two weeks, your voice will change automatically and you *will* be speaking with authority.

Let me give you an example of how a part of the famous "I Have A Dream" speech by Dr. Martin Luther King, Jr. would sound first, if it were delivered in a flat, unexciting, monotone voice, then with authority.

"I am not unmindful that some of you come here out of great trials and tribulations. Some of you have come fresh from narrow jail cells. Some of you have come from areas where the quest for freedom left you battered by the storms of persecution and staggered by the winds of police brutality. Go back to Mississippi, go back to Alabama, go back to South Carolina, go back to Georgia, go back to Louisiana, go back to the slums and ghettos of our Northern cities, knowing that somehow this situation can and will be changed.

Let us not wallow in the valley of despair. I say to you today my friends, that in spite of the difficulties and frustrations of the moment, let freedom ring. Let freedom ring from every hill and molehill along the Mississippi. From every mountain side, let freedom ring. And let it ring from every village and every hamlet of every stage and every city. Free to be able to speed up that day when all of God's children, black men and white men, Jews and Gentiles, Protestants and Catholics will be able to join hands and sing in the words of the old Negro Spiritual, "Free at last, Free at last, Thank God Almighty we are free at last!"

Now let's review that same segment of Dr. Kings's wonderful

speech and see how it would sound when it's spoken with *vitality, authority* and *energy!*

"I am not **unmindful** that some of you come here out of **great** trials and tribulations. Some of you have come **fresh** from narrow jail cells. **Some of you** have come from areas where the **quest for freedom** left you **battered** by the storms of persecution and **staggered** by the winds of police brutality. **Go back** to Mississippi, **go back** to Alabama, **go back** to South Carolina, **go back** to Georgia, **go back** to Louisiana, **go back** to the slums and ghettos of our Northern cities, knowing that **somehow** this situation **can and will be changed.** Let us **not** wallow in the valley of despair. I say to you **today** my friends, that **in spite of** the difficulties and frustrations of the moment, **let freedom ring. Let freedom ring** from **every** hill and molehill along the Mississippi. From **every** mountain side, **let freedom ring.** And let it **ring** from **every** village and **every** hamlet of every stage and every city. Free to be able to **speed up that day** when **all of God's children, black men** and **white men**, **Jews** and **Gentiles**, **Protestants** and **Catholics** will be able to **join hands** and sing in the **words** of the old **Negro Spiritual**, **"Free at last, free at last, thank God Almighty, we are free at last!"**

Can you see the difference in how key words are emphasized? This is how a person speaks with authority.

Now that you know how to improve this aspect of work related communication, try it out for several days. You will notice some people react differently while others are totally oblivious to what's going on around them. Keep working on this skill and you will have more opportunities come your way than you can imagine.

If you are speaking with authority at work you're well on your way to developing a **GREAT VOICE!!**

In Chapter Six, we will review how you can Create A New Phone Voice!

Chapter Five Notes

_____

_____

_____

_____

_____

_____

_____

_____

_____

_____

_____

_____

_____

_____

Chapter Five Notes

Chapter Six

Creating Your New Phone Voice

You have five seconds to make a favorable impression on the phone. In this chapter, you will learn to conquer the second biggest fear that limits many business people-speaking on the telephone. Also, I want you to become aware of the impact of your voice and *instantly* make a favorable impression to set more appointments, close more deals, gain more clients and earn more money.

If you use the phone extensively at work, this chapter will be extremely valuable to you. No longer will you mumble, bumble and stumble when presenting yourself on the telephone. These skills will *significantly* impact your performance in getting your point across quickly and effectively. You will *immediately* hear a change in the way people respond to you on the telephone.

Have you heard this type of call before?

Ring, Ring -   *Goo afererno, XYZ encyclopedee coomapnee, john, hep ya?*

Customer -   "Excuse me?"

Company Rep - *"XYZ encyclopedee coomapnee, john, hep ya?"*

Customer -   "Is this the XYZ Company?"

Company Rep - *"uh-huh."*

Customer -   "This is Jim Doe speaking. I placed an order several months ago for a set of encyclopedias and I'm starting to get concerned that I haven't received them yet."

Company Rep - *"hunh."*

Customer -   "Could you check on that for me please?"

Company Rep - *"unh-huh. Could you hold?"*

Customer -   "I suppose."

Five minutes and twenty obnoxious customer service commercials later —

Company Rep- *"Wha was yur name again?"*

Unfortunately this scenario happens every day, yet companies wonder why they are losing customers. You have a great opportunity to increase your sales, business and personal relationships by using the telephone properly. In this chapter, you will find a set of self-analysis questions to guide you through the process of developing great phone mannerisms and a great phone voice.

Remember that almost everyone you call during the business day has a busy environment and an incredible workload. For this reason, have all the necessary documents in front of you before you make the calls. Record your side of at least five phone calls. Analyze each one for several characteristics. Remember the regional and gender characteristics we discussed last chapter? The telephone magnifies them. If you are talking to someone from another part of the country regularly, focus on their regional and gender characteristics and list which ones you find distracting. There is a good chance that those same characteristics are evident to them as they listen to you! So you have a starting point.

Next, listen to your recordings and determine what would annoy or distract you if you were an outsider calling into your office. This list is not limited to region or gender. Let's begin the self-analysis. Use this as a guide to review your practice tapes. With some awareness, practice, review and application, you will probably be able to improve your phone habits quickly.

Action Assignment-

Answer the following questions-

1. Do I mumble into the phone?

_____

2. Do I speak in a monotone voice?

_____

3. Do I sound disinterested, or am I genuinely interested in speaking to the other person?

_____

4. Do I have good phone habits?

_____

5. Do I play with papers and other things in my office or am I totally focused on that conversation?

_____

6. Do I identify myself clearly and distinctly when I answer the phone, or do I mumble the name of the company, department or division, and fail to identify myself?

_____

7. Do I have the information that I need before I make a phone call to someone either in my company or outside the company?

_____

8. Am I using good grammar and language when I speak on the phone?

_____

9. Am I getting to the point quickly, or am I rambling and beating around the bush in order to make my point to the listener?

_____

10. Do I sound like a leader on the phone (someone the listener would perceive as a leader), or am I very submissive on the phone?

_____

11. Do I sound like I have self-confidence when I speak to someone on the phone, or am I very weak and self-limiting when I project my voice to the listener.?

_____

12. Am I speaking in my proper range of tonality, rather than too high or too low?

_____

13. As a woman, do I speak like a girl, or do I speak like a mature woman?

_____

14. As a man, do I speak with authority, or do I lack an authoritative sound, such as a casual 'I don't care' tone of voice?

_____

15. Do I mumble such monosyllabic words as 'yep, nope, uh-huh' or do I speak with flowing dialog?

_____

16. As a leader, do I tend to speak in a condescending tone to employees, or do I showthem appropriate respect as I speak to them on the phone?

_____

17. As a leader, do I ask someone to do something, or do I tell someone to do something in a very abrasive way?

_____

18. Do I thank people for taking my calls, for their time or for calling me?

_____

19. Do I speak with vivid imagery, or am I using trite sentences, words and phraseology that could be misconstrued or cause disinterest for the listener?

_____

20. Do I use a lot of slang or profanity when I speak on the phone? If so, what purpose does it serve?

_____

21. Do a use a lot of technical jargon when speaking on the phone to a non-technical person?

_____

22. Do I diminish suffixes when I speak on the phone or am I enunciating each word distinctly?

_____

23. Do I have a neutral voice when I speak to someone on the phone, or is there a noticeable regional accent that I would like to diminish or eliminate?

_____

24. Can my listener gain valuable information from me during a brief phone conversation?

_____

25. When I leave a message on someone's voice mail, is it too verbose or is it concise?

_____

26. When I leave a message for someone to return my call, what incentive do I give them?

_____

27. How many newspaper and magazine articles or passages in a book have I read onto a practice tape this week to help me improve my phone voice? (Note dates and #)

_____

28. Aside from monetary gain (if I'm on a commission basis), what rewards will I have aa person as a result of improving and creating my new phone voice?

_____

29. If there were one aspect of my phone voice that I could change, it would be _____

_____

30. If there were one aspect of my phone voice that I am proud of, it would be _____

_____

Review these questions on a regular basis to keep you focused on your best possible phone voice. You will hear immediate results when you follow these guidelines.

You should be projecting a happy, not harried or bothered image. We all enjoy talking to people who are very pleasant sounding on the phone, don't we? This is another opportunity for you to stand out from the crowd. Most people do not sound all that pleasant on the phone. If you display the characteristics covered in this chapter, people will want to become better aquainted with you. These new phone voice habits will reward you both professionally and personally. If you have already have a significant other, just talking to them using these secrets will give them a thrill! If you are not currently in a relationship, you will be soon!

Develop and display more energy on the phone by standing up while talking, especially at work. At least sit straight up in your chair. This prevents you from getting too lazy while on the phone. Since you are make progress through this book, you are becoming aware of the sound of your own voice as well as other people's voices. Simply use the poor speakers as warnings of what *not* to do. Please use encouragement to help some of them. Get into the habit of helping other people rise to new levels of achievement.

Now that you have learned the Secret of Creating Your New Phone Voice, you're well on your way to developing a **GREAT VOICE!!**

Next, we will cover the Secret of *Finding The Power To Be More Assertive!!*

* I conduct fun, informative seminars for telemarketing, customer service and sales organizations. You can reach me at the address in the back or call 1-800-989-2013 for more information.

Chapter Six Notes

Chapter Six Notes

_____

_____

_____

_____

_____

_____

_____

_____

_____

_____

_____

_____

_____

_____

Chapter Seven

Finding The Power To Be More Assertive

This breathing secret will have you ready for the challenge of speaking, with *reserve power!* In this chapter, we are going to talk about shedding the image of self-doubt about your ability to project your voice and stop trailing off at the end of sentences. I addressed this issue previously in Chapter Three because it is so prevalent in today's society. First, we will look at a graphic representation of a person trailing off at the end of sentences. Then we will see graphically how a person sounds with the *power* throughout the entire sentence. As you read the contrast of these two styles, listen to your own practice speaking tape and notice if you are trailing off at the end of sentences. The breathing ability that you are about to learn will help you project your voice throughout <u>entire</u> sentences each time you speak.

The following is a graphic example of how a presentation on the topic of recording equipment sounds when the person trails off at the end of words and sentences. Read it aloud and trail off where indicated.

All of the processing electronics are stored in external racks. The mic, or line racks are available in banks of sixteen channels that will select between mic or line input. These can be positioned on the studio floor or remotely in the machine room.

Can you see how the voice is trailing off at the end of the sentences? What this conveys to the listener is that you do not have total interest in your subject. By the way, your listeners analyze your voice subconsciously. If a person consistently trails off during a presentation or a conversation, listeners eventually lose interest.

Often this happens when a person presents by reading a script or copious notes. That's why I always train my students to get away from reading their notes during speech class. Notes are for REFERENCE, not public recitation. Do not read to an audience. Instead, speak in a conversational style. Your delivery style should be conversational, not monotone and stiff. When a person presents with the elements of monotone, stiff reading of a script, and trailing off at the end of sentences, it's no wonder people tune them out and get that glazed-over look. Let's not do this! You want to make an impact!

Now let's look at that information again and see how certain words and phrases to emphasize as we speak with *reserve* power. Read it aloud, bringing your volume and emphasis *up* on the bolded words.

"All of the processing electronics are stored in **external racks**. The mic, or line racks are available in banks of sixteen channels that will select between **mic or line input. These** can be positioned on the studio floor or remotely **in the machine room**."

Action Assignment-

Now I want you to get one of your favorite magazines, chose an article and read it into your tape recorder. Dissect the article by reading one sentence at a time in each paragraph. As you read the first time through, purposely trail off at the end of each sentence. Then read with increased strength at the end of each sentence, so that you completely enunciate the suffixes of those words. You may even underline certain words to remind yourself to emphasize them. If you felt out of breath after the exercise, keep reading.

Develop assertive speaking through the power of breathing. Most of us have poor breathing habits. Hear the good news! We can begin to improve our speaking with a simple breathing exercise. When can we do this? Practice in the morning while preparing for the day, or when you are at a traffic light. Do this while you are waiting in line at a restaurant or bank (don't worry, they will give you plenty of opportunities to wait in line). (?!)

First, locate the bread basket, which is also known as your breathing diaphragm. Just like exercising your biceps and other muscles in a gym, we have to develop the strength of this muscle. Hold your hands so that the palms are towards your chest with the fingertips touching. Place your hands on the diaphragm. Ladies, this is just below the lower part of your brassiere. Men, if you're wearing a brassiere, it's in the same place. If not, it's just above the rib cage. Take a deep breath, then exhale very slowly through your mouth while pushing on your bread basket. It will feel funny and you won't have much air to expel initially. That's O.K. You will get use to it and will get better as you build up your diaphragm, which is our goal in doing this exercise. Set the book down and do it now.

How did you do? If you did not do it, please put the book down NOW and do the exercise! Remember, knowledge is only half power. ***Knowledge put into action is full power!***

Go ahead. I'll wait. *Now*, how did you do? Do this one more time, counting to ten as many times as you can as you exhale. Ready? Take a deep breath, placing your hands where on your bread basket. Exhale slowly through your mouth and count repetitions of ten. Eventually you will be able to do five or six reps of or count to fifty or sixty by doing this exercise. You can make this a fun activity by involving children, yours or the neighbor's. They love to play along. Use your imagination and have prizes for the person that can count the highest number of reps, the person who can make the silliest faces, etc.

The next step is combining the reading and bread basket push to help you practice pushing out the words. At the end of your sentences, give your bread basket a little extra push to force the air out, helping to emphasize those last few words. Do this quick exercise anywhere you have a few minutes. Your breathing system will naturally develop this ability, just as muscle training will increase the strength and endurance of a person's arms and legs. Eventually your system will automatically respond to the challenge of speaking, without running out of breath. It will feel funny at first, but you will notice the improvements in your health as well. Why? Expanded breathing will help your circulation and energy. You will not feel or *sound* tired. In fact, you'll notice this even more as you develop your speaking voice. How many people sound tired to you when they speak, in person and on the telephone? Quite a few people fit into this category. If you have been one of them, this secret will help you begin a whole new life.

Now that you have the Secret of **Finding The Power To Be More Assertive,** apply that power and continue developing a **GREAT VOICE!**

Next, in Chapter Eight, we will explore *Becoming A More Effective Leader!*

Chapter Seven Notes

_____

_____

_____

_____

_____

_____

_____

_____

_____

_____

_____

_____

Chapter Seven Notes

Chapter Eight

Becoming A More Effective Leader

Have you ever wished for better understanding at work? All of us have, I'm sure. When you use the potent combination of voice and word inflections, the results are better understanding and more cooperation at work. This Secret should help you minimize costly delays and give concise instructions every tome you speak.

When a business leader steps up to the front of the boardroom and says 'Let's have our weekly staff meeting,' or 'Let's discuss the Johnson project,' he or she has a prime opportunity to use their voice and speaking mannerisms to take that meeting to the next level in effective communication. Have you ever attended a meeting where the boss just sits there grumbling, mumbling grunting and being less than encouraging? This situation can be frustrating. The focus in this Chapter is to use your voice and speaking mannerisms to become an encouraging leader and specifically, a better discussion leader.

When you speak with clarity and purpose in meetings or when giving directions, the listener(s) will pay closer attention to what you are saying. By using more inflection, you will also give them more inspiration to complete the task at hand. People often tell me about a boss that has treated them harshly. Either they embarrass them in front of their peers or they bark at everyone like no one deserves any respect. In this busy, downsized business world, it's east to see how a leader could blow up every now and then. What we want to accomplish in this chapter is how to choose and use words and voice inflections to give employees incentives to perform at high levels.

One of the best things I learned early in life was how to treat someone with kindness at work. I also learned from some of the classic supervisors how *not* to treat employees. I once worked at a Shell Service Station when I was young. Back then, most unskilled workers were treated pretty badly. Not at this station. Letton Banta, Jr, the owner and operator, was one of the kindest, most encouraging people I have ever met. He treated every employee like they were somebody. We would do just about anything for him as a result.

Here's the way it worked for him and can work for you. He asked people if they wouldn't mind doing something instead of standing around and barking orders. He could have done that too. Most service station owners did operate that way. Not only could he have done it, but he had plenty of experience as a U.S. Marine! However, he had us doing things that other station owners only dreamed about. When weren't too busy, he would say "Young Man, if you don't mind, would you go out there and clean up the parking lot of debris? When you're finished, if you don't mind, take one of those buckets of white paint and paint around the edge of the gas pump islands and the curb around the edge of the parking lot." What did we say? " Yes sir, Letton. I'll take care of it right away." Results? One of the cleanest, nicest, friendliest and busiest gas stations in the city. He made more money and got awards year after year for cleanliness and production in the entire country!

All that to say that his leadership style was very effective. I also had bosses that yelled, screamed, threw things and basically stressed everyone out with their poor communication skills. Then there are some bosses that are communicate through grunts and groans, like cavemen. Just remember, your voice and mannerisms have a significant impact on your employees' perceptions and performance. We can choose to work on this area of communication or continue to have communication breakdowns.

Here's your Action Assignment-

Ask yourself "How would my staff and crew describe me to someone else?" Do this on a daily basis to keep yourself in check.

Let's focus on word inflections. This means that you put life in to certain words and phrases as you convey your instructions and ideas to the employees. Inflection is defined as "modulation of the voice; change in pitch or tone of voice." Try using voice inflections with the highlighted words in the following sentence:

"**George**, if you **don't mind**, would you take **those** boxes from the pallets, **stack** them over against **that wall**, and check back with me when **you are done**?"

How did you sound? Record yourself reading this sentence and play it back until you hear a significant difference in the way you are emphasizing those words. Next, take an article fro the newspaper, highlight or underline action verbs and key nouns, (such as a person's name), and read it into the recorder. Note the date and time of each recording session. Continue doing this until you start to hear some significant change in your voice.

Apply these principles in the workplace and you'll see a big difference in how others react to you. Record what happens when you try something new.

Your employees, peers and bosses will recognize you for your efforts, which means that you are using your voice to become a more effective leader. You are on your way to developing a **GREAT VOICE!!**

*In Chapter Nine, we will discuss **Improving With AGE!!***

Chapter Eight Notes

Chapter Eight Notes

Chapter Nine

Improving With AGE!

You are Improving With AGE! Articulation, Grammar, and Enunciation! In this chapter, we will be using AGE to master the Secrets of Broadway acting to end mumbling, stop diminishing suffixes, and whip your lips into shape. You will learn mouth aerobics that any doctor would approve!

How are your skills at articulating ideas quickly and effectively? Can you think on your feet and answer a question thrown at you with little or no preparation? This is a little like asking if you can hit a baseball each time it's thrown. Sometimes, with practice and coaching, you will be able to hit it. Other times, you will strike out. Hey, even Babe Ruth struck out a lot. One of the best things you can do is improve your batting average as it relates to the field of communication. In this instance, I will be your batting coach. I want you to picture your five worst case scenarios and write them down. It could be that the big boss is coming in from Cleveland and asks *you* to give her a tour and status report of your department. Maybe your company has a client that has been difficult to please, but he spends a lot of money on your product and services, so everyone puts up with him. This time, it's your turn to make a presentation to him and his staff of ninnies. You could be up for a promotion and it hinges on whether you can stand the grilling of a panel of upper management during your upcoming performance review. Whatever you can think of, please take the time to write them down now.

How long is your list? You should have at least five case scenarios that you may be called upon to demonstrate your articulation skills. Now go back and prioritize each one, starting with number one as being the easiest and number five as being the hardest. After you complete this, write out a typical list of questions that could be posed to you during each situation. It's impossible to know everything, but list at least five of the most likely questions that would be asked. Next, get a family member or friend to role play the part of the questioner. For a panel, get a few friends together on the weekend for a cookout. Now, write the questions on index cards and give them to your questioner(s). Have someone time you so that you learn to respond intelligently in one to two minutes. It's amazing how some people ramble on without saying anything significant. If you do this, ask you family member or friends to coach you to be more specific.

At first, these practice sessions may frustrate you, but they can be fun and are essential for you to become more articulate in conveying your ideas. Stay on a weekly session for at least three weeks. After this time, you should really see some improvement. For some, it will be evident sooner, but give yourself three weeks just to be sure. You will start to build your abilities and confidence, while your peers who don't improve in this area take antacid tablets when the boss shows up unexpectedly.

The next step is to get several types of ideas running through your mind. Actors and actresses have a habit of reading a magazine or script aloud each morning to engage in a free flow of ideas from their minds to the audience. So, start doing this for only three to five minutes at first. Choose an article from your favorite magazine three mornings a week and read it aloud. You can read it to someone or by yourself, whichever situation you're in at the moment. This lets you process information quickly, since it's already written out for you, like a script. When you have completed this exercise, move to fiction books. They are a little harder to interpret at first, but the ideas you will start developing in your own mind will be incredible. Get a journal and write them down. As you begin reading the books, choose only two pages at a time to avoid fatigue.

By focusing on this exercise, (reading aloud), you are improving your articulation skills, which will be evident to you and others in meetings and presentations. Eventually, write a word or phrase on ten index cards and practice reciting a response to each card without the help of notes. One of the most liberating things you can do is get away from a heavy reliance on notes. Once I started doing this, my presentations got better and better,and yours will too.I always coach my speech students to attain this level of ability. Set a goal date to accomplish this, then enter the next speech contest if you are a member of Toastmasters International. If you are not a member, write me or call (714) 858-8255 for more information. It will change your life. If you speak professionally, as I do, you may feel this is beneath you. Get a grip. This is one of the best and least expensive ways to sharpen your skills, and I have seen some fellow professional speakers that needed all the help they could get. Besides, you can take the time to help mentor someone else for professional speaking. You'll make a lot of life-long friends, share a lot of laughs and hear interesting and entertaining speeches. What fun!

Now let's go to the next level, working on grammar, which is the Second Secret of Broadway acting. Improving your grammar will help you make a favorable impression upon your audiences every time you speak. The misuse of grammar is prevalent in our society today, primarily because we use a lot of slang. Many of us do not make a continued effort to expand our vocabulary on a regular basis. We can change.

The most frequent violations of poor grammar that I hear in my students' tapes are dangling prepositions. For instance, if a person says the sentence "Where's it at?" -"at" is a dangling preposition. It does not need to be at the end of that sentence. Therefore, "Where is it?" is a complete sentence. If you are speaking like that, you need to stop doing it *immediately* because that's an example of poor grammar. Another frequent use of poor grammar is the phrase "Ain't got no....." 'Ain't' is a word that has filtered into American society and is even in the dictionary. If you are in a storytelling situation and are painting the picture of the character for your listeners, that's acceptable. In business presentations, speeches, seminars and church events (such as a Sunday School class or a sermon), or a courtroom, you should not be using poor grammar. I am appalled at the number at the number of people who have poor grammar. Most people seem reasonably educated. These are just poor grammar habits they have developed over the years. Unfortunately, they don't know how bad they sound. Please begin working on your grammar *now.*

Another typical grammar violation that I hear in adults and children is "Me and Johnny went to the store" or "Me and Sally and the kids went to the ball game last night." Do you see what is happening here? They begin the sentence with the word "Me" when they are talking about themselves and someone else. Again, grammar is everything when you are making presentations. You can look like an Ivy League graduate with a high quality voice. However, if you get up and say "Me and Sally's been workin' on this presentation for three days and we ain't got no help from the accounting department. Now we think we can probably try this presentation for you today.' We had some handouts and I had a pen that I wanted to use, does anybody know where it's at?"

Blatant violations like these will not impress the boss. I assure you that the rest of your listeners will not be impressed either. Some listeners will subconsciously say (This person has made quite a few grammatical errors and I hope their presentation is better than what I just heard.) You have to be your own grammar police. As you are speaking in everyday conversations and catch yourself using dangling prepositions or slang, you need to stop yourself. What happens if you continue to use improper grammar every day? Those poor habits become harder to break as they become stronger in your life. Therefore, to break those habits, stop-in mid-sentence if you have to, and self-correct until the new way of using grammar becomes your habitual mode of speaking. We learned these behaviors, so we just have to learn better behaviors to replace them. Where did we learn them?

In some instances, as children, we have poor grammar because we mimic our care providers who may have limited grammar themselves. Hey, most parents who grew up during W.W.II went to work at a very young age, and therefore did not have the opportunities we have today. Without a love for books, audio and video cassettes, college, technical schools, adult education classes and seminars, we stifle our own language, comprehension and communication skills. The great news is that we do not have to continue in this mode of living. Just because a person has not been an avid reader or attended classes for the past five years does not mean that they have to act the same for the next five years. Do you know how long it takes to change? You can change in an instant. We don't have to spend a lot of time in therapy discussing why we have or have not developed this habit. We just have to change a little bit each day until new habits are formed. The same is true about our speaking voice. Just a subtle change each day until we have new ways of speaking.

Let's go to the next level and focus on the Third Secret of Improving with AGE, Enunciation. One of the fun things we did as children was pretend and make funny faces. Can you recall those days of pretending you were a fish swimming in the ocean? These mouth aerobics are full of funny faces to help your lazy lips get into shape. We have lazy lips as a by-product of our busy schedules. That is why we slur our words and diminish suffixes. After you start doing these exercises, you will stop those old habits.

As we get into the fun of the exercise of mouth aerobics, I want you to know exactly what to do. So grab a headband, get that aerobics tape (mine, if you have it. If you don't, call or write to us.), throw a towel around your shoulders and get ready to have some fun!

The first one is the **'Goldfish'**. If you will, make the face of a fish. How? Bring your cheeks in and get a real puckered, exaggerated look. Yes, you can use your hand to pull your cheeks into your mouth. You may need your hands to help you initially. There you go. Begin moving your mouth up and down as you squeeze with your hand. You can eventually hold it in without squeezing. Get kids in on this, they will love it. Act just like when you were a kid and you made a fish face. Your mouth is kind of puckered when you bring in your cheeks. Wiggle your lips up and down for the Goldfish effect. So when you see 'Goldfish,' that's the face I want you to make. This exercise works those areas of your upper and lower mouth that you normally do not use. Can you feel the burn? Okay. Let's move on.

The next one will be the **'Grandpa.'** That's where you bring your upper and lower lips over the edge of your teeth, just as a Grandpa would do if he wasn't wearing his dentures. You probably had a Grandpa that did this all the time. I am going to have you move your mouth up and down as you see the numbers 1, 2, 3, 4, etc. Do this so you will look like a Grandpa. You can even get a little hunched down or something. Have some fun with this exercise. As I call Grandpa, that's the face I want you to imitate. Remember to pull your lips in between your teeth, as if you don't have any teeth.

The next one will be **'Whoa Nelly.'** We put our little fingers from both hands in the corners of our mouth. (Make sure you wash your hands first.) Pull back, just like on a horse's reins and say 'Whoa Nelly.' Just pull those corners back. I know that it looks and sounds silly, but it is fun! This is a great way for you to wake up those tired, out of shape mouth muscles. We've got to whip those lips into shape!

Next, we are going to do a fun **'Jaw'** exercise. Put your hand on your jaw and just go from side to side and say **'Side to Side, Side to Side'** while moving your jaw. Hold it loosely and push it from side to side. Then drop it down, and give it that scared actor look. You know how they have those scenes where people are frightened- 'AHHHHHH.'!!'' When you say **'Open,'** just open your mouth as far as you can-then say **'Close'** and close it. Then go 'Open, Close, Open, Close,' and 'Side to Side, Side to Side.'

Next will be the 'Blowfish.' Take a deep breath, puff your cheeks out as much as you can and hold the air in your mouth. Push the air in both cheeks to the left, right, left, right. Just hum along with the aerobic music and you may find that Middle Third! Push the air into that jaw left and right. Bounce that back and forth. This helps the top, outer cheek muscles wake-up! They are asleep because we normally don't use that part of our face in everyday conversation.

Then we will go back and repeat the cycle. You can mix it up, but you get the idea. It's going to be 'Goldfish, Grandpa, Whooo Nelly, Jaw-Left-right, Side to Side, Open-Close, and then Blowfish. Are you with me? Great!

You've got to have fun with this! You can't say, "How stupid!" This is a great workout to do while at aerobics or just wearing your Walkman. Okay! Let's try it with the music. Put on that headband! Put on that aerobic outfit! Here we go!

Goldfish 1-2-3-4-5-6-7-8-9-10
Grandpa 1-2-3-4-5-6-7-8-9-10
Whooo Nelly-2-3-4-5-6-7-8-9-10
Jaw 1-2-3-4-5-6-7-8-9-10

This exercise works those areas of your upper and lower mouth that you normally do not use. Can you feel the burn? Okay. Let's move on Left-right, side to side, left-right, side to side, open, close

Whoa Nelly-2-3-4-5-6-7-8-9-10
Jaw 1-2-3-4-5-6-7-8-9-10
Jaw 1-2-3-4-5-6-7-8-9-1
Blowfish 2-3-4-5-6-7-8-9-10

Goldfish 1-2-3-4-5-6-7-8-9-10
Grandpa 1-2-3-4-5-6-7-8-9-10
Whoa Nelly-2-3-4-5-6-7-8-9-10
Jaw 1-2-3-4-5-6-7-8-9-10
Left-right, side to side, left-right, side to side, open, close
Blowfish 2-3-4-5-6-7-8-9-10

Goldfish 1-2-3-4-5-6-7-8-9-10
Grandpa 1-2-3-4-5-6-7-8-9-10
Whoa Nelly-2-3-4-5-6-7-8-9-10
Jaw 1-2-3-4-5-6-7-8-9-10
Left-right, side to side, left-right, side to side, open, close

Blowfish 2-3-4-5-6-7-8-9-10

Goldfish 1-2-3-4-5-6-7-8-9-10
Grandpa 1-2-3-4-5-6-7-8-9-10
Whoa Nelly-2-3-4-5-6-7-8-9-10
Jaw 1-2-3-4-5-6-7-8-9-10
Left-right, side to side, left-right, side to side, open, close
Blowfish 2-3-4-5-6-7-8-9-10

Goldfish 1-2-3-4-5-6-7-8-9-10
Grandpa 1-2-3-4-5-6-7-8-9-10
Whoa Nelly-2-3-4-5-6-7-8-9-10
Jaw 1-2-3-4-5-6-7-8-9-10
Left-right, side to side, left-right, side to side, open, close
Blowfish-3-4-5-6-7-8-9-10

Cool down. Did you feel the burn? Now you are ready to speak, because now you have mouth muscles that you have never used! You can be alive, alert, awake and enthusiastic! Now, go out and try to read something! Give a speech. Talk to someone and you will find that this little exercise in the morning or anytime you can do this. You can do this in your car! This will really entertain your fellow motorists on the highway! Do this at the red light. Put that tape in and have fun with this! This will help you improve your enunciation and your speaking voice. You *do* want to improve, don't you?

We can have a lot of fun with a mouth aerobics exercise. Take a few minutes and cool down. Now let's focus on how to stop diminishing suffixes. When we learn this Secret and practice it every day, it's easy. Here's an example of diminishing suffixes: Secretar' William Perry wen' to Capt'l Hill to star' wha' is li' to be a proces' of consultatio' with Congress on the shape of the new mission. After listenin' to Perry, my judgmen' is that there will be a bipartisa' consens' to suppot' the Pres's decisn' provid' that there are clear limi's on tha miss'n to be performed by our troops and a spec' time line statd.' Accordn' to tha Pentegn' won' be lon.'

Could you see that I was diminishing the suffixes? We also have a tendency to diminish suffixes ending in "ing." In research, I found that they are the most prevalent suffixes dropped or diminished. Sometimes the "tion" ending or suffix is diminished also.

Now let's try that again, without diminishing the suffixes. See if you can tell the difference. "The then secretary William Perry went to Capital Hill to start what is likely to be a drawn out process of consultation with Congress on the shape of the new mission. After listening to Perry's briefing, a senior republican and member of the Senate arms committee predicted that congress eventually would go along with the decision to take part in the follow up force. My judgment is that there will be a bipartisan consensus to support the president's decision provided that there are clear limits on the mission to be performed by our troops and a specific time line stated. According to the pentagon, the total cost of the mission by the end of this year will be $3.28 Billion more than 60% above the original estimate."

Could you see the difference between this and the previous paragraph? A conscious effort to bring the suffixes up on 'listening' and 'briefing' and saying each syllable of each word is necessary.

As you practice reading this, your speaking might sound a little halted on your practice tape. That's fine. Master this Secret of bringing up the suffixes up completely and work on the flow of the recording later. It will take a while for you to do this. We often speak rapidly and diminish those suffixes. especially the "ing" ending suffixes. Those are the most diminished suffixes in the English language. Work on this by reading a newspaper, magazine or favorite book- analyzing the words. Look at their structure. Look at the syllable structure and make sure that you do not diminish those suffixes in your practice session. You will hear a few suffixes diminished at first, because we do this naturally. As you practice speaking at a lower rate of speed, you will bring the end of the suffix up and eliminate the tendency to diminish those key words. Practice this exercise three times a week. You will hear improvements in your voice in the second week of doing this exercise.

Let's review the principles in Improving With AGE-Articulation, Grammar and Enunciation. We started out with articulation, writing questions to your five most difficult things to handle. Reading aloud each day will also help you as it does Broadway actors and actresses. Then we reviewed how to improve your grammar, by keeping it in check, being aware of some of the most common violations and getting study material on grammar, such as <u>Word Power</u> by Charles Ickowicz. Finally, we did the mouth aerobics to help you with enunciation or speaking more distinctly. You should be able to recognize and eliminate the habit of dropping the 'g' on 'ing' ending words. Other dropped suffixes include 'tion' and lead to diminishing suffixes. By selecting a newspaper or magazine article and underline key words, you can work on multiple syllable words and diminished suffixes. Then you can record the reading without diminishing the suffixes to practice full enunciation.

As you go through your morning rituals every day, practice these principles. You will see and hear a tremendous difference in your presentations, and in the way that you improve your reading as you read aloud in the practice sessions. Other people will see and hear the difference and they will say *"Gosh, you sound great!" What will be your response? "Thank you very much. I'm Improving With AGE!"*

This means that you are well on your way to developing a **GREAT VOICE!!**

In the next chapter, we will discuss **Putting Family Traditions Into The History Books Forever!**

Chapter Nine Notes

_____

_____

_____

_____

_____

_____

_____

_____

_____

_____

_____

_____

_____

Chapter Nine Notes

Chapter 10

Putting Family Traditions Into The History Books Forever

We can break free from mispronounced words, limiting dialog, stereotypical slang and weak sentence structure. I chose family traditions as the theme of this chapter because all of these characteristics can contribute to being an ineffective communicator. As I briefly mentioned in Chapter Nine, our vocabulary stems from the people that surround and care for us as we grow from infancy into adulthood. These people usually include our parents, grandparents, aunts, uncles, baby-sitters, friends and teachers. I call them care providers. They help shape our lives more than we will ever know. For the positive influences, let's be thankful. For the negative influences, let's learn how the bad vocabulary habits we developed may be preventing us from achieving greatness.

As we develop in the teen stages, we become more influenced by our peers, friends, higher education faculty and the media, including television and movies. In this chapter, we will review how you can overcome some of the family traditions that *may* be holding you back both professionally and personally. Words and phrases such as "you know, huh, um, ain't got no, Me and Sally went to ..., It don't make no difference, Where's it at?" These are just a few examples of trite and incorrect phrases. Eliminate them.

My esteemed colleague, Dr. Elaine Friedrich states "If you are using these trite phrases, you run the risk of coming across to the listener as having a limited vocabulary. These skills test a person's social graces as well. Picture this. You are talking to someone at a social function and as you try to engage them in conversation, they only say "Yeah, huh, beats me." It will not be long before you are looking for someone else to talk to, even if it means finding the kitchen help to discuss meal preparation. Do you recall business or social situations where it's been difficult to get someone to speak fluently? Sure you do. This happens all the time. Why on earth have not these people improved their social skills? They have accepted the status quo.

As a result, these people will experience minimal success because of the traditional limited vocabulary and lower self-esteem that stems from several family traditions. Hey, if you worked as hard as Uncle Joe works at the factory, engaging in meaningful conversation would be difficult too. Turn off that television set and go to work on breaking that family tradition *right now!*

Here's Your Action Assigment-

This exercise will help you to assess those words that you use unconsciously, such as; "you know," "O.K.," "uh-huh," "ain't got no" and the others mentioned above. Then we will review some new words to replace some of the old words you want discard.

Find a magazine you like to read, perhaps from home. You probably have at least two magazines lying around the house. If you are like me, you subscribe to several magazines. These are wonderful tools to help you develop the expansive dialog we have been discussing. I want you to take a magazine, put on your practice tape and choose an article to read onto the tape. First, read the article aloud several times (Note: choose a short article!) Turn the recorder on and read it for your practice session. I want you to focus on the way the words sound as they come out of your mouth. Spend about 20 minutes reading this article. You will need to use vocal vitality, variety, and emphasis. What will this do for you? This will help you develop an expansive dialog, our focus in this chapter. By doing this exercise, you will start putting these words and phrases into your memory bank. The more you read, the more expansive your dialog is going to be. It's simple and painless.

How does slang interfere with our ability to communicate effectively? Again, let's hear from a communications expert, Dr. Elaine Friedrich. "Several factors come to mind. If the listener doesn't understand a particular word (slang or technical jargon), then they feel left out. This does not communicate good feelings between the speaker (you) and the listener. Our mission when we speak either one-on-one or in front of a group is to connect with the listener(s).

Record yourself in everyday conversation, either speaking face to face or on the phone. Play the tape back and count the number of slang, filler, technical or swear words that you use. You may be using more than five inappropriate words in a ten minute conversation. If the most prevalent words are slang, they are in your presentations too. Let's put a stop to that. Just count and record which words are slang, filler, technical or swear words. Identify them by category: (1) family, (2) your peer group, (3) regional, (4) work or industry, etc. Feel free to make as many categories as you can think of to help you improve.

Continue this list, noting every slang and/or swear word that comes to mind. (You could be there for a while!) Using a check mark, note which words you think you are using too frequently. Next, sit down with a friend and ask *them* to help you identify the slang, technical, filler or swear words you use too frequently. Review this list daily to bring the words from your subconscious to your conscious mind and minimize or eliminate them in your daily communication. Keep a small journal notebook to make it convenient to carry. This activity will take a little time, but you will begin to see the results quickly.

Another key area I want to address is the use of word substitution. These are words that could be slang derivatives or words that have a similar sound but different definition altogether. The word "gonna" is slang for "going to" and "wanna" is slang for "want to," for example. I call these examples lazy slang, because it does not take much effort to say them, while you have to exert a little more effort to say the correct phrase. If we want to sound our best, we will break out of this very distracting habit. Other word substitutions have crept in to the American vocabulary include, but are not limited to: "dis, dat dem" and "dos" for "this, that, them" and "those."

How do you think slang words sound to listeners in your presentations? They may not tell you personally, but I will. These words do not impress listeners. How do you know if you are using them? Record yourself talking on the phone, in casual conversations, meetings or presentations. As mentioned in the earlier exercise, this method of capturing your voice will give you the tally and frequency of each word. Awareness is the first key to improving your speaking voice. The more you know about yourself, the more you can correct certain behavior characteristics. Just like a professional athlete, you are trainable. You can use these principles for self-coaching. All it takes is a positive mental attitude to be on your way to success. Are you with me? Great! Let's continue.

An excellent way to diminish or eliminate filler words such as "you know," "O.K.", "Uh," "um," "like" and any other filler is to say a sentence or talk for 5 minutes a day with someone while constantly saying the word or phrase. Here is an example. "By, you know, applying the above principles, you know, to your speech, you know, you'll find that a good speaking voice, you know, generally has the, you know, following characteristics, you know." Does that drive you crazy or what? People who use filler phrases often sound this excessive. Write out a sentence or paragraph, incorporating the word or phrase you want to eliminate. Read the words back twelve times while recording yourself.

Play the tape in the car while you are driving- *alone*. Play the tape in your Walkman while working out or walking. You probably will not be able to stand it too much more after this, but it *will* reinforce the new behavior and you will diminish or eliminate this irritating word or phrase from your vocabulary! The temptation to convert other people will be strong! It's funny that we have let these words creep into our vocabulary, and often do not become bothered by their repetitive use until we do this type of exercise.

As you work on these skills, you are developng a **GREAT VOICE!!**

*In Chapter Eleven is the **Secret of A Bore No More!***

Chapter Ten Notes

_____

_____

_____

_____

_____

_____

_____

_____

_____

_____

_____

_____

_____

_____

Chapter Ten Notes

_____

_____

_____

_____

_____

_____

_____

_____

_____

_____

_____

_____

Chapter 11

A Bore No More - Eliminating Monotone Habits!

Have ever been to the Atlanta International airport or any major metropolitan airport and taken the tram (the little shuttle train that takes you from one concourse to the next)? If so, you've heard the mechanical voice say "Stop! We are about to leave the station. Please move to the center of the train and away from the door. Next stop is Concourse A." The voice is monotone because it is computerized. How many people do you hear talk like this on a daily basis? My guess would be 'Quite a few.'

The sound of this voice is reminiscent of the old space movies where the Martians landed on earth, pointed their ray guns and said "Take me to your leader." If you speak with a monotone voice you are boring (and losing), your audience. Having a monotone voice is the most common violation of spoken communication.

We will review the sound waves and tonality continuum from Chapter Two again because this concept is important in eliminating a monotone sound. When a person has a monotone voice, they will consistently speak above or below the continuum in flat, unimaginative tones during an entire presentation or conversation. Audiences fade because they are falling asleep! They are craving something else more exciting! On the bright side, this Secret will help you improve your voice almost immediately.

I have great news! You can eliminate a monotone sound by studying and developing melody in your voice through; (1) **awareness** (2) **coaching** (3) **practice exercises** and (4) **application.**

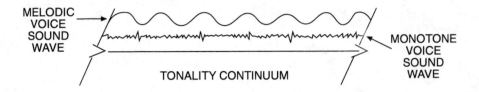

Action Assignment-

Practice this exercise when you are at a red light or while waiting for someone. We actually have a lot of idle time on our hands waiting on people or events. Get into the habit of taking something to read or do while you wait for others.

This following information is paraphrased from an actual AP newswire. When I was a broadcaster on Armed Forces Radio, Associated Press bulletins would come across the news teletype and we would read them at the top of the hour. First, read in a very flat, monotone sound. Then read with melody, emphasizing key words. The point of this exercise is to help you to develop natural melody by emphasizing key words.

"This just from the news wire: Astronomers are elated over the collision of the comet Schumaker Levy 9 with the planet Jupiter. Fragments of the comet began striking the gigantic planet last night. Professional grade telescopes have been gathering pictures. Comet co- discoverer, Carolyn Schumaker said that everyone hit the ceiling when we heard the results. She calls the results, "Too exciting to believe.""

Her husband, Eugene, also a co- discoverer, says there have been reports that smaller telescopes also had detected second long flashes. They spoke at a news conference at Goddard Space Flight Center in Maryland. Four fragments already have hit the planet, with more hits expected."

A Bore No More! Eliminating Monotone Habits

If you read that in a low key, monotone voice to an audience, your listeners would be asleep by now. Let's try it again with some ***melody*** and ***excitement*** in your voice!

From the AP wire in Greenbelt, MD: Astronomers are **ELATED** over the collision of the **COMET SHOEMAKER LEVY NINE** with the planet Jupiter. Fragments of the comet began **STRIKING** the gigantic planet last night. Professional grade telescopes **HAVE BEEN** gathering pictures. Comet co-discoverer, Carolyn Schumaker said that everyone **HIT THE CEILING** when the results came in. She calls the results **"TOO EXCIT-ING TO BELIEVE!"**

Her husband, Eugene, also a co-discoverer, says there have been reports that smaller telescopes also have detected **"SECOND-LONG FLASHES!"** They spoke at a news conference at **GODDARD SPACE FLIGHT CENTER** in Maryland. Four fragments already have hit the planet, with **MORE HITS** to come. With the latest from the Associated Press, I'm _____! (your name here)

Do you see the melody there? Can you hear the melody as you emphasize the highlighted words? This type of exercise will help you break monotone tendencies quickly and easily. Practice this exercise now using your tape recorder to capture your voice. Ready? Go!

Another fun type of practice is reading the sports scores. Even if you don't care for sports, this is a great exercise. If you can make something you don't care about exciting, just think how exciting your voice will sound about one of your favorite topics! Sportscasters on television and radio use a lot of inflection and place high emphasis on certain teams, scores and plays. You can do this too, with a little practice. Since these are old scores, don't despair if your favorite teams didn't win! First, read this in a flat, monotone style to give you a sense of average speaking!

"Now turning to baseball, in the National League; the final scores are:

Atlanta over Florida, 2 to 1
San Diego slammed the New York Mets, 10 to 1
Houston shut out Pittsburgh, 9 to 0
San Francisco topped Montreal, 9 to 7
The Cardinals lost against Colorado, 10 to 6 and
Cincinnati beat the Cubs in 10 innings, 3 to 2

In the American League; the final scores are

Milwaukee over Minnesota, 5 to 3
The Chicago White Sox beat Cleveland, 5 to 2 in the bottom of the ninth,
Baltimore doubled California, 10 to 5
It was Boston edging out the Oakland A's, 4 to 3 in a close game and
the Yankees pummeled the Seattle Mariners, 14 to 4 in New York
In the top of the sixth, currently it's Kansas City, 4, Detroit, 1 and
the Toronto Blue Jays lead the Texas Rangers, 2 to 1 in the bottom of the
7th.

That's the baseball roundup, I'm _____ (your name here).

Did you do that with a flat, monotone sound? Good. Now read it again, emphasizing the highlighted words, using the rhythm of music as a cadence background. Regardless of your interest in sports, act like you LOVE BASEBALL! Remember to choose some fast paced music from a tape (maybe one of mine), a CD or the radio to serve as a background.

NOW TURNING TO BASEBALL!
IN NATIONAL LEAGUE ACTION TODAY, *HERE* ARE THE FI-NAL SCORES:

ATLANTA over Florida, 2 to 1
It was San Diego **PUMMELING THE NEW YORK METS, 10 TO 1**
Houston **BLANKED** Pittsburgh, 9 to ZIP!
It was **SAN FRANCISCO** over Montreal, 6 to 4
Philly **BEAT L.A.** in a **CLOSE MATCH,** 9 to 7
Colorado **OVER** St. Louis, 10 TO 6
In 10 innings, the Chicago Cubs **FINALLY** lost to Cincinnati, **THERE, 3 to 2**

In the **AMERICAN LEAGUE,**

It was **MILWAUKEE** over Minnesota, 5 to 3
The **CHICAGO WHITE SOX TOPPED** Cleveland, 5 to 2 in the bottom of the ninth
Baltimore **DOUBLED** the California Angels, 10 to 5 and
the **YANKEES SLAMMED** Seattle, 14 to 4.

In the Top of the sixth, it's **KANSAS CITY OVER** Detroit, 4 to 1 and the Toronto Blue Jays **LEAD** the Texas Rangers, 2 to 1 in the bottom of the 7th. **THAT'S THE LATEST** from the AP wire, I'm _____ (your name here).

Can you see and hear the melody here? Can you hear yourself emphasizing the key words? This exercise will HELP you eliminate monotone habits. Now do this again while recording yourself on a practice tape. Remember to mention the date each time you begin a new practice session.

Next, let's review some history.

A History of American Law
by
Lawrence Friedman (copyright 1973)

Judicial review of state statutes was a rare, extrordinary event in 1850; it was a common occurance in 1900. What happened in the state courts paralleled what happened in the federal courts. The taste for power was even more intoxicating to state tribunals. The figures speak loud and clear. In Virginia, for example, up to the outbreak of the Civil War, the state's high court had decided only thirty-five cases in which the constitutionality of a law or practice was questioned.

Of these, the court declared only four unconstitutional. Between 1861 and 1865, "A dozen or more laws or practices were declared unconstitutional." The Alabama Supreme Court went so far as to declare the entire constitution of 1865 null and void. The real spurt, however, came at the end of the century. In Minnesota, the Supreme Court declared nineteen laws unconstitutional in the 1860's.

Only thirteen statutes fell in the next fifteen years. But between 1885 and 1899, approximately seventy state statutes were struck down, with a decided bunching in the last few years of the century. In Utah, between 1896 and 1899, twenty-two statutes were reviewed by the Utah Supreme Court. Exactly half of these were declared to be mere parchment and ink.

Are you asleep? Now let's read this with a STRONG EMPHASIS on the highlighted words. This exercise works best if you are stand ing up , using a lot of ANIMATED BODY LANGUAGE! You'll really have an impact on your performance if you present it to a group. This can be really funny if you have two groups taking turns presenting it. If you do it the way that I want you to, you will be exhausted by the end! This illustrates that we can bring the most dry information to life. So, if we can do this, we should be able to break free from a dry monotone voice when we present something we can get excited about. Let's go over this again, this time with as much energy and enthusiasm as you can physically give. I want you to stretch a bit to make this exciting. Are you with me?! Here we go!

JUDICIAL review of state statutes was a **RARE, EXTRAOR-DINARY** event in 1850; it was a **COMMON** occurance in 1900. What **HAPPENED** in the state courts **PARALLELED** what happened in the federal courts. The **TASTE** for **POWER** was even **MORE INTOXI-CATING** to state tribunals. The figures speak **LOUD** and **CLEAR.** In Virginia, for example, up to the outbreak of the **CIVIL WAR,** the state's **HIGH** court had decided only thirty-five cases in which the constitutionality of a **LAW** or practice was questioned.

Of these, the court declared only **FOUR** unconstitutional. Between 1861 and 1865, "**A DOZEN** or more laws or practices were declared **UNCONSTITUTIONAL.**" The Alabama Supreme Court went so far as to declare the **ENTIRE** constitution of 1865 **NULL AND VOID.** The real **SPURT,** however, came at the **END** of the century. In **MINNE-SOTA,** the **SUPREME** Court declared nineteen laws **UNCONSTITU-TIONAL** in the 1860's.

Only **THIRTEEN** statutes fell in the next **FIFTEEN** years. But between 1885 and 1899, approximately **SEVENTY** state statutes were **STRUCK DOWN,** with a decided **BUNCHING** in the last few years of the century. In **UTAH,** between 1896 and 1899, **TWENTY-TWO** statutes were reviewed by the **UTAH SUPREME COURT.** Exactly **HALF** of **THESE** were declared to be **MERE** parchment and **INK.**

How did you do? Ha! Have some fun with these so you are working to Elinminate A Monotone Voice and develop a **GREAT VOICE!!**

*Now it's time to learn about the **Rewards Of A Storyteller's Voice!***

Chapter Eleven Notes

_____

_____

_____

_____

_____

_____

_____

_____

_____

_____

_____

_____

_____

_____

_____

Chapter Eleven Notes

Chapter Twelve

Gaining The Rewards Of A Storyteller's Voice

Are you a storyteller? What makes a good storyteller? There are several factors. Expanding your talents in speaking by using voice inflections and language to paint vivid images for your listeners will make you a great storyteller. We all love stories. There's nothing like hearing a good story told well. If you are a speaker, seminar leader, teacher, minister or historian, you know the power of a good story. That's why novels, movies and TV are so popular. Even more rewarding than being a spectator is to be the storyteller.

There are some key things that we must do to be effective, though. Just getting up and reciting a story from its printed form is not enough. We need to maintain the ancient art of relating events and beliefs by using various speaking talents to enhance the story for our listener(s). Just imagine the days before electronic media, (TV, radio, etc.) One of the ways people got news in the land was by storytellers. Some stories became largely exaggerated and stirred emotions beyond the relative significance of the events. Even today, the media tends to sensationalize stories to keep our interest high. Let's review the positive aspects of storytelling.

There are at least ten secrets of an effective storyteller. (1) Charisma-the teller should have a pleasing personality to be likable by the audience. (2) Sense of humor- having the ability to laugh and make people laugh helps make a strong connection between you and your audience. You don't have to be a stand-up comedian, but a little humor goes a long way. Most everyone loves a good laugh, unless they were weaned on a pickle. (3) Imagination-to be a successful storyteller, you need to paint the scenes of the stories in your own mind's eye so you can share them with your listeners. To stimulate this very important characteristic, turn off the TV and read more books. (4) Getting into character-voice inflections and speaking mannerisms will take you to a higher level of speaking and entertaining your audience. Study actors and actresses in plays to see how they portray different characters. Also, remember how you played different grown-ups when you were a kid? Let's be kids again and get into the character(s) of the story. Remember Robin Williams in Mrs. Doubtfire! Ha!

(5) Having the ability to use the environment is key. You don't need an elaborate stage setting to be effective. Using a few natural and man-made props will go a long way to helping you paint the picture for the audience. For instance, if you are outside, you may be able to use a tree, rock, hill, stream or any other aspect of nature. Inside, you can use a chair, window, door, light-switch, desk or other physical features of the environment. Also, to portray a character you may use hats, canes, jackets, pipes, glasses or other simple items to help stimulate the imagination. I know some people insist that props aren't necessary. It's a difference of opinion and there are plenty of opportunities for all styles of storytelling. Do what you feel comfortable with and don't limit yourself. Your audience will appreciate anything you can do to help them enjoy the presentation.

(6) Having the ability to use vivid imagery to paint the picture in the mind's eye of the listeners is also important. I will say this again and again. When you develop this ability, the world is your audience. A good speaker will work hard to master this trait. Your voice inflections, combined with what I call 'word crafting', will transform a weak presentation into a strong one. Two people who had this trait were Dr. Martin Luther King, Jr., and Earl Nightingale. Listen to these two masters of the spoken word to get an idea about how you can develop this ability. Review Dr. King's speech again and see the vivid imagery in print. With a little research and practice, you can also become very good. More on how to develop this ability in the Action Assignment. (7) Voice-it should be melodic and rich in tonality (Review Chapters Two and Eleven), as you tell

the story. Characterization may call for a different sound, but your audience will stay with you easier when you have melody and richness. (8) Having the ability to keep an audience attentive. This is a real challenge today because of the hectic lifestyles we lead, forty-seven channels on cable and new Nintendo games for kids every six months. You can keep them attentive by being alive and 'setting the stage' for each scene with descriptive narration. This ability may take a while to develop. Your mind's eye is the key here. Imagine the scene, then share that image with your listeners. If you can, use the voice characterizations we spoke of in number four.

(9) The ability to use facial expressions and gestures. We have so many talents that we habitually fail to use. In telling a story, your face can portray all the emotions and move an audience to laughter or tears. When combined with the words of the story and the proper voice tonality, your face and body gestures will pull the audience into the story and keep them there to the end. Practice with a partner to develop all the facial and body gestures to display joy, sadness, love, anger, surprise, fright and fun. Your audience will respond to you in a very powerful way.

(10) Audience participation-if there was one thing that took my speaking to the professional level, this was it. You can do it too. Many people have not learned this secret and fail to effectively connect with their audiences. If you do not get anything else from this book, this secret should make it worth the price. How do we get audience participation? There are several ways. One of the techniques I found to work best, especially in storytelling, is to do what I call 'scene enacting.' Ask a member of the audience to come up on stage or in front of the audience and help you demonstrate a scene or role play a situation. If you have not rehearsed this, it's even better.

I recently conducted a seminar and did a scene enactment with a member of the audience, with no prior rehearsing. The scene was a job interview, and all I told him ahead of time was to be as zany as he could be, and I would portray the straight laced interviewer. Did it work? It brought the house down! People were falling out of their chairs, they were laughing so hard. I had a hard time staying in character myself. He was so witty and the scene enactment went so well that people asked me later if we had reheased it. Your audience *wants* you to be successful and will be glad to take part in activities that are fun. Make it a major goal to begin audience particiation with your next presentation.

These ten secrets of a great storyteller will help build your self-confidence and put you in high demand as a speaker. I belong to the National Storytelling Association. You can join a local chapter in your area and go to the annual Fall festival in Jonesborough, Tennessee to hear some great storytellers. People from all walks of life are there to share their stories and techniques. For more information call (423) 753-2171.

When you see people sitting in their chairs, waiting on the next thing you say about the story, it's rewarding. Maybe they are laughing because you are able to change your voice to sound funny and portray a character in the story. Kids love this and will endure many hours of sitting and listening to a good storyteller. Whatever you can do make the story interesting, your audience will love you. Developing a storyteller's voice will be a good time for you and for your listeners.

Again, as a storyteller, paint the picture of the story in the minds eye of the listeners using vivid imagery, voice inflections and voice characterizations.

What do we know about storytelling?

- It is still the preferred way of conveying information between people, regardless of age.

- A good 'teller' is able to effectively craft words and phrases to paint vivid images for the listeners.

- Use of voice characteristics helps the listeners to better understand the character's modus operandi, or the way they think and present themselves.

- Convincing an audience of the story's validity is accomplished by confining proper gesturing, content, occasional props and a well trained voice.

- Folklore, fables, fact and personal experiences are all around us, so the storyteller never runs out of material to share with an audience. There are many types of stories. The range includes, but is not limited to: historical, mythological, inspirational, humorous, entertaining and ghost stories. With any of these types of stories, you can hold an audience's attention while helping them develop their creative minds.

- Using a lot of theatrical abilities with your natural voice in a storytelling mode lets you do some acting while giving your listeners an opportunity to see themselves in the story.

- A dull, boring business meeting can be PEPPED UP using stories to illustrate key points. People who do this successfully get more participation, more results, more sales and get promoted quicker than their peers who are sullen, boorish, sarcastic, argumentative or introverted. Every time. Try it.

One of the best ways to interact with children is to get them to use their imagination to help you tell the story. Remember, I said help, not take over. If you haven't had much experience with this, here's a friendly warning. Kids are hams, for the most part. They will take over if you let them. Also, if you are 'telling' to a classroom full of kids, they will ask you all kinds of questions and say things out of the blue that have nothing to do with the story. This could throw you off track, but a little preparation will help.

I was once 'telling' children in a Sunday School class about the Bible lesson when a sweet little five year old girl blurted out "My Mommy wears green lipstick!" Without missing a beat I said, "So the Disciples were traveling along the Nile, where Cleopatra wore green lipstick when she was Queen of Egypt. The Disciples couldn't cross the river so they went towards the city ......" and finished the lesson. She later whispered loudly to her friend "My Mommy's like Cleopatra!, the Queen of Egypt!" Ha! They are just *so* innocent. Be prepared to stay on the storyline. More on this and other subjects in my forthcoming book The Storyteller's Way, which is due out in late Fall 1997.

Children love stories and I highly encourage you to virtually memorize a story and take it to new heights as you become the 'teller' of the tale. Try to use different voice characterizations for each character in the story. The kids will love it! If you don't have any kids, entertain the neighbor's kids or volunteer at your local library. They will love you for taking the time to do it.

If you or anyone in your organization is interested, I conduct speeches, seminars, and customized voice and communication training for executives, telemarketing, customer service call centers and phone companies. All training is highly interactive and fun! Contact my office for more information about my schedule or other products and services at 1-800-989-2013.

Mentor someone starting today.

Finally, just remember this:

ONE OF THE MOST POWERFUL THINGS THAT CAN EVER BE SAID ABOUT YOU IS THAT <u>YOU HAVE A GREAT VOICE</u>!!

Make something wonderful happen today!

All The Best,

Michael W. Hall, DTM, CSL

Chapter Twelve Notes

_____

_____

_____

_____

_____

_____

_____

_____

_____

_____

_____

_____

_____

_____

Chapter Twelve Notes

Chapter Twelve Notes

_____

_____

_____

_____

_____

_____

_____

_____

_____

_____

_____

_____

_____

_____

_____

For more information about ordering this book on audio, or for other product or services, please call 1-800-989-2013 or fax 1-901-755-1083. Quanity book discounts are available. All orders will be shipped within 48 hours.

You may also write for a free catalog to:

CCI
PUBLISHING
"Leaders In Progressive Publishing"
1-800-989-2013
www.cci4pros.com

Name _____
Address (No P.O. Boxes, please) _____
City _____ State _____ Zip _____
Business Phone (____) _____
❑ Check (Payable to CCI Publishing) ❑ P.O. # _____
Credit Card: ❑ Visa ❑ MC ❑ AMEX
Cardholder's Name _____
Card Number _____ Exp. _____
Signature of Cardholder _____
Total Order S _____
In TN add 8.25% sales tax or provide tax exempt number _____

Convenient Ordering Methods: Call us toll free at: 1-800-989-2013, or you may fax your order to: (901) 755-1083 or mail this form with payment / P.O.# to: CC I Publishing • 676 Germantown Parkway • Suite 538 • Cordova, TN 38018
Thank You for your order - A percentage of the proceeds will benefit St. Jude Children's Research Hospital!

CCI Publishing's Hot New AudioBook Series!
Resource Information & Order Form

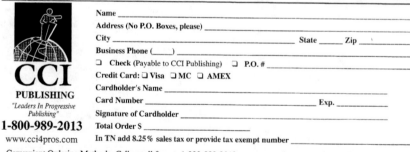

About CCI Publishing -
We are committed to providing high quality audiobook programs to educate, inspire, entertain and motivate the listener through dynamic, innovative seminars and studio sessions. We believe that knowledge put into action is power, so each program comes complete with action assignments and coaching by the authors. Our authors are professional speakers delivering current and cutting edge information to help the listener improve the quality of their lives. As people lead more fast-paced, hectic lifestyles, they can enjoy the convenience of listening to these programs in their car, while exercising or in the comfort of their home. All products are unconditionally guaranteed. These audiobooks are a great addition to innovative resource libraries!

"Twelve Secrets Of A Great Voice" is a complete course with guidebook in a beautiful 10" x 12" hard bound case. Approx. 5 1/2 hours. "Recruiting Christian Leaders with E's" is an ideal audio/text seminar in an attractive guidebook. Approx. 4 hours. All single programs are in a handsome 4-1/2" x 7" case. All titles are ready for display and circulation.

Save!! Purchase the entire series and save 15% Save!! Receive 15% discount on orders over $200.00. Free audio for orders over $100 before Apr. 18 , 1997.

Title	Price	Qty	Total
"Twelve Secrets Of A Great Voice" *A practical guide for enhancing your presentations, career and life!* Michael W. Hall, 6 Audio Cassette Course & Guidebook ISBN 1-890432-01-6	$59.95		
"Creating Your New Phone Voice" *Enhancing your telephone image to instantly make a favorable impression.* Michael W. Hall, ISBN 1-890432-02-4	$11.95		
"Interview Skills & Self-Marketing Strategies For Success" *Preparing to seek new employment, higher positions, or new clients.* Michael W. Hall, ISBN 1-890432-03-2	$11.95		
"Valentine's Day & Other Ways To Train Men" *Strategies to empower women so courtship isn't just about tennis.* Pamela L. DeLong, ISBN 1-890432-04-0	$11.95		
"The Big "D"- Dating In The 90's & Other Natural Disasters" *Why we play the game and how women can make up all the rules.* Pamela L. DeLong, ISBN 1-890432-05-9	$11.95		
"Leadership, Management & You" *Innovative ways YOU can improve your company's effectiveness.* Michael G. Blain, ISBN 1-890432-06-7	$11.95		
"Glimpses Of Heaven" *Spiritual insights of life after life.* Elaine Friedrich Hall, ISBN 1-890432-11-3	$9.95		
"Recruiting Christian Leaders with E's" *Developing lay ministry in your congregation.* Elaine Friedrich Hall, 4 Audio Cassette Course & Guidebook ISBN 1-890432-16-4	$59.95		
Grand Total			

Shipping & Handling Charges For Guaranteed Delivery

Orders Up to:	Add:
$39.99	$4.95
$40.00 to $79.99	$5.95
$80.00 to 139.99	$7.95
$140.00 to 199.99	$9.95
$200.00 to 499.99	$13.95
Over $500.00	$24.95

Additional Address Handling Charges
Items sent to more than one address add $3.00 each additional shipment.

CCI
PUBLISHING
"Leaders In Progressive Publishing"
1-800-989-2013
www.cci4pros.com

Name _____

Address (No P.O. Boxes, please) _____

City _____ State _____ Zip _____

Business Phone (_____) _____

❏ Check (Payable to CCI Publishing)   ❏ P.O. # _____

Credit Card: ❏ Visa ❏ MC ❏ AMEX

Cardholder's Name _____

Card Number _____ Exp. _____

Signature of Cardholder _____

Total Order $ _____

In TN add 8.25% sales tax or provide tax exempt number _____

Convenient Ordering Methods: Call us toll free at: 1-800-989-2013, or you may fax your order to: (901) 755-1083 or mail this form with payment / P.O.# to: CC I Publishing • 676 Germantown Parkway • Suite 538 • Cordova, TN 38018

Thank You for your order - A percentage of the proceeds will benefit St. Jude Children's Research Hospital!